MEDIEVAL LATIN LITURGY

A SELECT BIBLIOGRAPHY

TORONTO MEDIEVAL BIBLIOGRAPHIES 9

General Editor: John Leyerle

Published in Association with
the Centre for Medieval Studies, University of Toronto

RICHARD W. PFAFF

Medieval Latin Liturgy
A SELECT BIBLIOGRAPHY

UNIVERSITY OF TORONTO PRESS
Toronto Buffalo London

© University of Toronto Press 1982
Toronto Buffalo London
Printed in Canada

ISBN 0-8020-5564-8 (cloth)
ISBN 0-8020-6488-4 (paper)

Richard W. Pfaff is a member of the Department of History at
the University of North Carolina at Chapel Hill.

Canadian Cataloguing in Publication Data

Pfaff, Richard W. (Richard William), 1936-
    Medieval Latin liturgy : a select bibliography

(Toronto medieval bibliographies; 9)
Includes index.
ISBN 0-8020-5564-8

1. Liturgies — History — Bibliography. I. Title:
Medieval Latin liturgy : a select bibliography.
II. Series.

Z7813.P42   016.264   C82-094016-X

This book has been published with the help of a grant
from the Publications Fund of University of Toronto Press.

Editor's Preface

The study of the Middle Ages has been developed chiefly within university departments such as English or History. This pattern is increasingly being supplemented by an interdisciplinary approach in which the plan of work is shaped to fit the subject studied. The difference of approach is between Chaucer the English poet and Chaucer the civil servant of London attached to the court of Richard II, a man interested in the Ptolemaic universe and widely read in Latin, French, and Italian. Interdisciplinary programs tend to lead readers into areas relatively unfamiliar to them where critical bibliographies prepared with careful selectivity by an expert are essential. The Centre for Medieval Studies at the University of Toronto takes such an interdisciplinary approach to the Middle Ages, and the need for selective bibliographies has become apparent in our work. The Centre has undertaken to meet this need by sponsoring the Toronto Medieval Bibliographies.

In his valuable guide, *Serial Bibliographies for Medieval Studies,** Richard H. Rouse describes 283 bibliographies; the number is surprisingly large and indicates the considerable effort now being made to provide inclusive lists of items relevant to medieval studies. The total amount in print is already vast; for one unfamiliar with a subject, significant work is difficult to locate and the problem grows worse with each year's output. The reader may well say, like the throng in *Piers Plowman* seeking the way to *Treuthe,* 'This were a wikked way but who-so hadde a gyde' (B.vi.I). The Toronto Medieval Bibliographies are meant to be such guides; each title is prepared by an expert and gives directions to important work in the subject.

* Publications of the Center for Medieval and Renaissance Studies 3, University of California, Los Angeles (Berkeley and Los Angeles 1969)

Each volume gives a list of works selected with three specific aims. One is to aid students who are relatively new to the area of study, for example Medieval Celtic Literature. Another is to guide more advanced readers in a subject where they have had little formal training, for example Medieval Rhetoric or Latin Liturgy; and the third is to assist new libraries in forming a basic collection in the subject presented. Individual compilers are given scope to organize a presentation that they judge will best suit their subject and also to make brief critical comments as they think fit. Clarity and usefulness of a volume are preferred over any demand for exact uniformity from one volume to another.

Toronto, September 1981

JL

Contents

C
The Mass

D
The Daily Office

E
The Occasional Offices

H
Early Roman Liturgy and Derivatives

J
'Roman-German' Liturgy (c. 900-1200)

Author's Preface

In a series dealing with such a wide range of subjects as that covered by the Toronto Medieval Bibliographies, divergences of approach and even of detail are bound to be inevitable. The object of this preface is as much to indicate the approach which has informed the present volume as to explain such details as conventions of citation and the terminal date for items included. Such matters, of approach and detail alike, are important to a bibliography, so important that it would not be amiss to follow the practice of the eminent reference work which printed at the foot of each page 'Please Read Preface.'

Two factors make the pursuit of medieval liturgical matters rather different from many aspects of the study of the middle ages. The first is that to a large extent the subject is incomprehensible except in terms of the whole of the early Christian development which preceded it. The second is that, 'liturgics' being a branch of modern theological study, investigations of the medieval liturgy have often been coloured by theological preconceptions and ecclesiastical fashions: a desire for the recovery of authentic chant styles, for instance, or an emphasis on worship as the expression of *Mysterien-theologie,* or a concern to expand the laity's role in the services of the church. To some extent the same two factors have operated in the study of medieval monasticism, but in a much limited way: as Giles Constable's volume in this series has shown, it is scarcely necessary to trace Christian monasticism earlier than the late third century A.D., and theological concern with the monastic life is only part of the wider subject of Christian perfection or ascetical theology.

For our purposes, the two factors mentioned above must be taken as two cautions. As for the first, we must limit ourselves strictly to those sources for, and literature concerning, early Christian worship which cast light directly on the medieval liturgy. Fortunately, a recent book, *The Study of Liturgy*, ed. Cheslyn P. M. Jones et al. (London and New York 1978), provides a guide to early Christian worship (as also to the period of the Reformation and later) which is highly adequate for all background purposes. For the middle ages, however, its treatment is cursory, sometimes even superficial: of 141 pages on the liturgy of the eucharist, for example, only 21 are devoted to the medieval western rites. This brings in our second caution: the middle ages are not liturgically fashionable now, and the subject seems to deserve no more than passing attention from those who are concerned with 'liturgics.' So the student who needs to know something about the medieval liturgy will have not only to approach with care works dominated by theological concerns (whether of the old Roman Catholic-Protestant polemics or the modern ecumenical, and, one is tempted to say, monolithic Liturgical Movement), but also to go beyond the works of liturgical scholars to those of palaeographers, philologists, art historians, and other humanists.

Such elaborate cautions may seem scarcely necessary to users of this series; but the study of liturgy — unlike, say, that of medieval Romances — is so rooted both in a distant past and (for many of those engaged in it) in the living present that we cannot overstress that our study is in a strict sense historical: the history of the medieval Latin liturgy from the late fourth century (the earliest period we know anything to speak of about it) to the sixteenth-century Reformation.

In other respects the scope of this bibliography can be more simply delineated. It aims to cover the most important source-editions of and literature concerning the medieval Latin liturgy. The limit of roughly one thousand titles which is the normal maximum for this series means that if this aim is at all to be accomplished — problems of the compiler's inevitable subjectivity aside — it must be within some strict limitations. The first of these is that articles of less than ten pages have, with very few exceptions, been omitted arbitrarily, in the hope that such substantial value (often considerable) as they possess will have been incorporated in further studies. The second is that 'Latin' has been construed pretty strictly, so that references to, say, liturgical aspects of vernacular literature — the influence of the liturgy on such-and-such Anglo-Saxon poems — have been excluded.

Also excluded are the very numerous works where the theological purpose
is paramount or at least overshadows the scientific value; thus such well-
known titles as Gueranger's *Année liturgique* and Schuster's *Liber sacramentorum* will not be found here.

Any bibliography not organized simply alphabetically or chronologically
has an implied shape to it. In the present work this operates in two ways.
In the first place, my view of the history of medieval Latin liturgy is implicit
in the table of contents. Secondly, attention has been paid to ancillary
subjects in proportion to their immediate bearing on liturgical history.
Thus there are quite a lot of titles with musical interest (obviously requiring
some overlap with Andrew Hughes's excellent and extensive bibliography
in this series; nonetheless fewer than five per cent of the titles listed here
appear in his work) because much liturgical observance was sung. But aspects
of the liturgy which are primarily of dramatic or literary interest, or which
pertain chiefly to canon law or the minutiae of hagiography, are treated
scantily if at all. And it may be well to note that the words 'liturgy' and
'liturgical' are construed here in a deliberately narrow sense, to include only
that which bears on the performance of the liturgy. For example, medieval
treatises on the doctrine of the eucharist or modern works on the grades of
holy orders are excluded — a necessity again imposed by considerations of
size. Likewise excluded are paraliturgical topics such as vesture, furnishings,
and architecture. If a revised and expanded edition of this bibliography
should ever prove feasible, it might be possible to include such topics. For
the present all such fascinating byways (as also the decoration of liturgical
manuscripts) have had to be resisted.

That this work is limited to roughly one thousand titles will immediately
warn the user that its character is preliminary rather than exhaustive. What
may not be quite so obvious is that these titles are not presented as the
thousand 'most important' for the study of the subject, but rather as including the most fundamental work in the variety of periods, areas, and aspects
covered. Clearly some of these have been the subject of more scholarly
attention than others, whether justifiably or not; it follows that some quite
important studies of the Gregorian sacramentary, say, have had to be omitted so that any titles on something like the liturgy of penance could be
included.

So much for exclusion. In the direction of fullness, an attempt (not
always successful) has been made to list one review for monographs and
editions published since 1960. (The inclusion of older books suggests in

itself that they have some enduring value.) And I have tried not only to
indicate English translations of sources and monographs where such exist,
but also to list a few admittedly elementary works in English. For more
advanced items, I have assumed that it is realistic to include titles in Latin,
French, German, Italian, and Spanish (including Catalan); Dutch, Portu-
guese, and the Scandinavian languages very rarely (there is often an English
summary in such works); and other languages not at all.

I have attempted to cover books and articles published through 1977
(i.e. in volumes of periodicals ostensibly dated 1977). The bulk of the
present bibliography was compiled in 1977 and 1978, and extensive reference to later titles has proved impossible.

It may be helpful if several details about conventions of citation are
clarified. Editions are cited under the name of the modern editor unless
the work in question is by a clearly identified medieval author, e.g. Amalarius
or John Beleth; *ordines* and regulations ascribed to a particular figure – like
Bernhard canon of the Lateran, Eberhard the cantor, or Lanfranc – are
likewise cited under the editor's name (in these cases, Fischer, Farrenkopf,
and Knowles respectively) but with separate entries in the index. Items
which are part of a numbered series have been so indicated, and an attempt
has been made to note reprints, though such information is probably far
from complete. Second and subsequent editions have been cited whenever
they incorporate substantial revisions, but multiple places of publication
only exceptionally. Place names are given in their most usual English forms,
with certain conventions employed throughout: Freiburg for the German
(Freiburg-im-Breisgau) and Fribourg for the Swiss centre of learning;
Münster *simpliciter* for Münster-im-Westfalen; Cambridge for the English
and Cambridge, Mass. for the American town; and no separate designation
for the Vatican City (in existence only since 1929) as opposed to Rome.
Titles are sometimes given in a shortened form, and lengthy subtitles printed
only when they contain important information. Throughout, conciseness
has been aimed at more than complete technical bibliographical detail.

As mentioned above, I have tried particularly to note translations into
English; works so translated are usually cited in their original form first,
but when the English version seems to have become the principal one (e.g.
Baumstark's *Comparative Liturgy*) that order has been reversed. Individual
articles from the big dictionaries and collaborative works listed in section A
are cited, or even cross-referenced, only when they are of unusual length or
importance. Essays reprinted in the collected papers of four masterly

scholars listed in **A4** (Edmund Bishop, Wilmart, Callewaert, and Jungmann) are cited as in those collections, with an indication of the date of original publication.

As in some other volumes of this series, an asterisk indicates that the item has not been seen personally by the compiler. Such items have, obviously, been kept to an absolute minimum.

On the question of the order in which items are cited in each section, helpfulness has been preferred to consistency. In general, where there is a definitive modern work this is given first, followed by a standard edition if one exists (very occasionally more than one). Then come editions, in ascending chronological order — earliest to latest — and studies, in the same order. But where the nature of the heading seems to demand a different order this has been followed. Specifically, within a heading like 'Anglo-Saxon' which includes a large span of time, items are arranged where possible not by order of publication but by the period they date from or refer to; while in large areas like 'French Local' an obvious order of locations has been employed. No standardized order has seemed as helpful as this flexible practice. The order of the items under every heading has been established with the aim of providing in each case the greatest assistance to the user.

Two further conventions, these about names, need explanation. The initials of religious order have been omitted as being unnecessary and, in these days of frequent changes, often inaccurate. And, secondly, I have tried to list the same person's name the same way — in its most usually encountered vernacular form — throughout. This has proved no small problem in the case of authors who publish in a variety of languages (is it Alexander, Alexandre, or Alejandro Olivar?) and who have taken names in religion: Stephen J. P. van Dijk published for a time as (S.) Aurelian van Dijk, and the prodigiously prolific Dom Mohlberg appears under many combinations of Leo, Cunibert and Kunibert, and their initials. In such cases a stern standardization has had to be imposed. It is more important that the searcher have some idea of the total accomplishment of important liturgical scholars (which the index of names should hint at) than that his path is made wholly plain at the card catalogue; and in any case library cataloguing practice files many of the items listed here under the infuriatingly general rubric of 'Catholic Church. Liturgy and Ritual.' Still, as an aid to using author catalogues, first names are given for authors of books (but not articles) — though there are a few who resist all attempts to pry beyond their initials.

The index is one of authors, including editors, wherever possible. The only titles indexed are those of periodicals and series. If a work has two authors or editors both are indexed; if more than two, only the editor or apparently predominant figure. Authors of book reviews are not included.

It should be noted that this is a bibliography of titles, not a repertory of liturgical manuscripts or an assemblage of materials towards a complete reconstruction of ancient liturgies. Outstanding works of both these types exist in more plentiful supply than do straightforward bibliographies such as the present effort. For the most part each title is cited just once. Cross-references (indicated by boldfaced numbers) are given for important references only; to provide a completely cross-referenced bibliography of this sort — including every reference to liturgy in the Spanish peninsula, for example, or to the canon of the Mass — would swell this volume out of all proportion and would serve no useful purpose. In consequence, it is strongly recommended that users of this bibliography familiarize themselves with its basic shape, as outlined in the table of contents.

Every bibliography has its limits; the more the user realizes the limits of this one, the more help it may offer.

ACKNOWLEDGEMENTS

Friends and colleagues too numerous to mention individually have helped with occasional suggestions. I owe thanks in particular to Susan Hicken and Rosalie Radcliffe for a careful job of typing; to the Institute for Research in Social Science for photocopying service; to the staff at the Wilson Library of the University of North Carolina - Chapel Hill, and above all to those in the Inter-Library Loan office, for ready and cheerful help in tracking down a large number of obscure items. My wife has kindly assisted with several checking tasks, each duller than the one before.

RWP

Abbreviations

AB	*Analecta Bollandiana* (**A.5.10**)
ACC	Alcuin Club Collections (**A.5.1**)
ALW	*Archiv für Liturgiewissenschaft* (**A.5.11**)
DACL	*Dictionnaire d'archéologie chrétienne et de liturgie* (**A.2.2**)
EL	*Ephemerides liturgicae* (**A.5.12**)
ET	English translation
HBS	Henry Bradshaw Society (**A.5.2**)
HS	*Hispania sacra* (**A.5.13**)
JEH	*Journal of Ecclesiastical History* (**A.5.14**)
JLW	*Jahrbuch für Liturgiewissenschaft* (**A.5.11**)
JTS	*Journal of Theological Studies* (**A.5.15**)
LQF	Liturgiegeschichtliche Quellen und Forschungen (**A.5.3**)
MHS	Monumenta Hispaniae sacra, serie litúrgica (**A.5.4**)
PL	Patrologia Latina, ed. J.-P. Migne (**A.5.5**)
R	Review (i.e. book review)
RB	*Revue bénédictine* (**A.5.16**)
RED	Rerum ecclesiasticarum documenta (**A.5.6**)
RHE	*Revue d'histoire ecclésiastique* (**A.5.17**)
SE	*Sacris erudiri* (**A.5.18**)
SF	Spicilegium Friburgense (**A.5.7**)
ST	Studi e testi (**A.5.8**)
TA	Texte und Arbeiten (**A.5.9**)
ZKT	*Zeitschrift für katholische Theologie* (**A.5.19**)

MEDIEVAL LATIN LITURGY

A SELECT BIBLIOGRAPHY

General

Bibliographies

Cf. Cross **A.2.1**, *DACL* **A.2.2**, Schmidt **A.2.14**.

A.1.1
Cabrol, Fernand. *Introduction aux études liturgiques* (Paris 1907)
To be used with utmost caution.
A.1.2
Vismans, Thomas A. and Lucas Brinkhoff. *Critical Bibliography of Liturgical Literature*, English ed. Bibliographia ad usum seminariorum E 1 (Nijmegen 1961)
Often useful but heavily directed towards the needs of Roman Catholic seminarians.
A.1.3
Hughes, Andrew. *Medieval Music: The Sixth Liberal Art.* Toronto Medieval Bibliographies 4 (Toronto 1974; rev. ed. 1980)
R: *Speculum* 52 (1977) 381-2: T.H. Connolly.
A.1.4
(Various authors). 'Literaturbericht,' *JLW* 1 (1921) - 15 (1935, publ. 1941), for the years 1914-35; esp. the section 'Die Liturgie des Abendlandes vom 4-15 Jahrhundert' by A.L. Mayer. This 'Literaturbericht' continues in *ALW* from 1 (1950); most years there are one or more extensive sections on medieval Western liturgy, e.g. in 2(1952) H. Frank, 'Entwicklung der abendländischen Liturgie vom 4. Jahrhundert bis 1000,' 133-97 and A.L. Mayer, 'Liturgie und kirchliches Leben im Abendland von 1000 bis 1500,' 198-337. Note also the frequently appearing sections entitled 'Monastische Liturgie' and 'Gregorianischer Gesang.' In recent years less space seems to have been devoted to the middle ages.

A.1.5
(Anonymous). 'Bibliographia liturgica,' *EL* 43 (1929) - 79 (1965). During World War II this bibliography appeared only in 54 (1940) and 58 (1944); the gap was caught up with special supplementary numberings in 60 (1946) and 61 (1947). From 80 (1966) there are 'Notae bibliographicae,' generally brief and pastoral in orientation, as the arrangement, which is according to the Constitution on Sacred Liturgy of Vatican II, suggests.

Dictionaries, Manuals, and General Histories

A.2.1
Cross, Frank L. and Elizabeth A. Livingstone, eds. *The Oxford Dictionary of the Christian Church.* 2nd ed. (Oxford 1974; 1st ed. 1957)
The indispensable starting-point, unmatched among one-volume reference works for breadth of coverage and accuracy.
A.2.2
Cabrol, Fernand and Henri Leclercq, eds. *Dictionnaire d'archéologie chrétienne et de liturgie.* 15 vols. in 30 (Paris 1907-53)
A vast compendium of information but always to be used with care, especially in the later, more hastily-compiled volumes.
A.2.3
Aigrain, René, ed. *Liturgia: Encyclopédie populaire des connaissances liturgiques* (Paris 1931)
A comprehensive and succinct treatment, but somewhat outdated in both approach and details.
A.2.4
Eisenhofer, Ludwig. *Handbuch der katholischen Liturgik.* 2 vols. (Freiburg 1932-3). From E's completion in 2 vols. (Freiburg 1912) of Valentin Thalhofer's *Handbuch*, I (1890), II never finished. For full bibliographical details see Schmidt **A.2.14**, 745.
A.2.5
Lechner, Joseph and Ludwig Eisenhofer. *The Liturgy of the Roman Rite,* ed. H.E. Winstone. ET (Freiburg and Edinburgh-London 1961) from '6th' ed. of *Liturgik des römischen Ritus* (Freiburg 1953), a revision of the '5th' ed. (1950), which is itself a reworking of Eisenhofer's *Grundriss der Liturgik des römischen Ritus,* 4th ed. (1937; 1st ed. 1924). The work is often cited simply as Eisenhofer's.

A.2.6
Righetti, Mario. *Manuale di storia liturgica.* 4 vols. 2nd ed. (Milan 1950-59; 1st ed. 1945-53)
This is often inaccurate, and must be used with great caution.
A.2.7
Dix, Gregory. *The Shape of the Liturgy* (London 1945)
This immensely influential work, concerned largely but not exclusively with the eucharist, has also been highly controversial; among important reviews are those of C.W. Dugmore, *JTS* 47 (1946) 107-13 and J.A. Jungmann, *ZKT* 70 (1948) 224-31.
A.2.8
Steuart, Benedict. *The Development of Christian Worship* (London 1953)
Heavily influenced by Dix, this book contains useful and concise summaries of the state of opinion (at its date) on a number of controversial points.
A.2.9, 10, 11, 12
King, Archdale A. *Liturgies of the Religious Orders* (London 1955); *The Liturgy of the Roman Church* (London 1957); *Liturgies of the Primatial Sees* (London 1957); *Liturgies of the Past* (London 1959)
Though these works will often be referred to below for the valuable information they contain, they are marred by an uncritical handling of sources and an inaccuracy of presentation.
A.2.13
Miller, John H. *Fundamentals of the Liturgy* (Notre Dame 1959)
Despite its title, quasi-encyclopedic in scope.
A.2.14
Schmidt, Hermanus A.P. *Introductio in liturgiam occidentalem* (Rome 1960)
Especially useful for analytical contents (often noted below) of several festschriften, volumes of collected essays, and series.
A.2.15
Radó, Polycarpus. *Enchiridion liturgicum: Complectens theologiae sacramentalis et dogmata et leges iuxta novum codicem rubricarum.* 2 vols. 2nd ed. (Rome 1966; 1st ed. 1961)
An enormous work; like Lechner **A.2.5**, primarily rubrical in orientation.
A.2.16
Martimort, Aimé-Georges, ed. *L'Eglise en prière: Introduction à la liturgie.* 3rd. ed. (Paris 1965; 1st ed. 1961). ET of pt. i as *The Church at Prayer: Introduction to the Liturgy* (New York 1968) and of pt. ii as *The Church at*

Prayer: The Eucharist (New York 1973); pts. iii and iv not translated
Helpful for the state of modern opinion on many aspects of the liturgy, but
primarily theological in tone.
A.2.17
Klauser, Theodor. *Kleine abendländische Liturgiegeschichte* (Bonn 1965).
ET as *A Short History of the Western Liturgy* (London 1969)
R: *Theologische Literaturzeitung* 92 (1967) 631-3: K.-H. Bieritz
Though extremely learned and full of striking insights, this is not a consecu-
tive history and is informed by the concerns of the modern liturgical move-
ment. An earlier form of the same work is *Abendländische Liturgiegeschichte*
(Bonn 1944); ET as *The Western Liturgy and its History: Some Reflections
on Recent Studies* (Oxford 1952).
A.2.18
Davies, John G., ed. *A Dictionary of Liturgy and Worship* (London and
New York 1972)
Slanted markedly in the direction of modern liturgical renewal.

History of Liturgical Scholarship

A.3.1
Mohlberg, Leo Cunibert (Kunibert). *Zeile und Aufgaben der liturgie-
geschichtlichen Forschung.* LQF 13 (Münster 1919)
A pamphlet packed with useful summaries.
A.3.2
Aigrain, René. 'Lexique des principaux liturgistes' in *Liturgia* (see **A.2.3**)
1033-88.
A.3.3
Leclercq, Henri. 'Liturgistes' in *DACL* (see **A.2.2**) 9.ii.1729-49.
A.3.4
Bouyer, Louis. 'On Liturgical Studies,' appendix (pp. 272-81) to his
Liturgical Piety (Notre Dame 1955). Repr. as *Life and Liturgy* (London
1956).
A.3.5
O'Shea, William J. 'Liturgiology,' *New Catholic Encyclopedia* 8 (1967)
919-27.
A.3.6
Rasmussen, N.K. 'Some Bibliographies of Liturgists,' *ALW* 11 (1969) 214-18,

15 (1973) 168-71, 19 (1977) 134-9. A third supplement is to be printed in the 1981 volume, along with a cumulative index.

Collected Essays and Festschriften

A.4.1
Bishop, Edmund. *Liturgica historica: Papers on the Liturgy and Religious Life of the Western Church* (Oxford 1918).
A.4.2
Wilmart, André. *Auteurs spirituels et textes dévots du moyen âge latin: Etudes d'histoire littéraire* (Paris 1932).
A.4.3
Callewaert, Camille. *Sacris erudiri: Fragmenta liturgica collecta ...*, ed. the monks of St. Peter's, Steenbrugge (Steenbrugge 1940).
A.4.4
Jungmann, Josef A. *Gewordene Liturgie: Studien und Durchblicke* (Innsbruck 1941).
A.4.5
Jungmann, Josef A. *Liturgisches Erbe und pastorale Gegenwart: Studien und Vorträge* (Innsbruck 1960). ET as *Pastoral Liturgy* (London 1962).
A.4.6
Capelle, Bernard. *Travaux liturgiques.* 3 vols. (Louvain 1955-67).
A.4.7
Miscellanea liturgica in honorem L. Cuniberti Mohlberg. 2 vols. Bibliotheca 'Ephemerides liturgicae' 22-3 (Rome 1948-9).
A.4.8
Colligere fragmenta: Festschrift Alban Dold ..., ed. Bonifatius Fischer and Virgil Fiala. Texte und Arbeiten, 1. Abteilung, 2. Beiheft (Beuron 1952).
A.4.9
Mélanges en l'honneur de monseigneur Michel Andrieu (Strasbourg 1956; = *Revue des sciences religieuses*, volume hors série).
A.4.10
Mélanges liturgiques offerts au R.P. Dom Bernard Botte O.S.B. ... (Louvain 1972).

Series and Journals

A.5.1
Alcuin Club Collections (London 1899-).
A.5.2
Henry Bradshaw Society (London 1891-).
A.5.3
Liturgiegeschichtliche (from 1957, Liturgiewissenschaftliche) Quellen und
Forschungen (Münster 1918-)
A conflation of Liturgiegeschichtliche Quellen, Heft 1-12 and Liturgie-
geschichtliche Forschungen, Heft 1-10, the latter being renumbered 13-22
of the consecutive series, which is united from 23 on. The consecutive (re)-
numbering is the one cited here. Listed through 34 (1958) in Schmidt **A.2.14**.
A.5.4
Monumenta Hispaniae sacra, serie litúrgica (Barcelona etc. 1946-).
A.5.5
Patrologia Latina, ed. J.-P. Migne. 221 vols. (Paris 1844-64).
A.5.6
Rerum ecclesiasticarum documenta (Rome 1950-). Series maior: Fontes.
Series minor: Subsidia studiorum.
A.5.7
Spicilegium Friburgense: Texte zur Geschichte des kirchlichen Lebens
(Fribourg 1957-)
There is also a 'Subsidia' sub-series.
A.5.8
Studi e testi [Bibliotheca Apostolica Vaticana] (Rome 1900-).
A.5.9
Texte und Arbeiten: I. Abteilung. Beiträge zur Ergründung des älteren
lateinischen christlichen Schrifttums und Gottesdienstes (Beuron 1917 -).

A.5.10
Analecta Bollandiana (Brussels 1882-).
A.5.11
Archiv für Liturgiewissenschaft (Regensburg 1950-). Continuation of
Jahrbuch für Liturgiewissenschaft (Münster 1921-35 [1941]).
A.5.12
Ephemerides liturgicae (Rome 1887-).

A.5.13
Hispania sacra (Madrid 1948-).
A.5.14
Journal of Ecclesiastical History (London 1950-).
A.5.15
Journal of Theological Studies (London and Oxford 1899-).
A.5.16
Revue bénédictine (Maredsous 1884-).
A.5.17
Revue d'histoire ecclésiastique (Louvain 1900-).
A.5.18
Sacris erudiri: Jaarboek voor Godsdienstwetenschappen (Steenbrugge 1948-).
A.5.19
Zeitschrift für katholische Theologie (Innsbruck and Vienna 1877-).

Liturgical Manuscripts

GENERAL

A.6.1
Dekkers, Eligius, with Aemilius Gaar. *Clavis patrum Latinorum.* 2nd ed.
(Steenbrugge 1961; = *Sacris erudiri* 3; 1st ed. 1951)
Pages 423-67 provide exhaustive guidance (including an *Elenchus codicum*)
to liturgical sources in Latin to c. 800; the basic working list of editions,
which every scholar must keep up to date for himself.
A.6.2
Gamber, Klaus. *Codices liturgici Latini antiquiores.* Spicilegii Friburgensis
subsidia 1. 2 vols. 2nd ed. (Fribourg 1968; 1st ed. 1963)
R: *AB* 87 (1969) 265-8: G. Philippart; *Rivista di storia della chiesa in Italia*
23 (1969) 490-98: B. Baroffio
The indispensable, though far from infallible, guide to Latin liturgical
manuscripts from the 5th through the 11th centuries.
A.6.3
Vogel, Cyrille. *Introduction aux sources de l'histoire du culte chrétien au*
* *moyen âge.* Bibliotheca 'Studi medievali' 1 (Spoleto 1966; 2nd ed. 1975*)
R: *Cahiers de civilisation médiévale* 9 (1966) 254-6: B. Botte

This massively detailed work of scholarship unfortunately omits virtually everything pertaining to the divine office.

CATALOGUES

This section is limited to six outstanding catalogues, all but one of them recent; obviously the catalogues of all collections containing Latin liturgical manuscripts would be relevant here. Cf. Leroquais **C.2.3, D.1.5, D.4.1, E.4.5, F.15.3**; Brückmann **E.4.7**; Hesbert **M.4.1**; Radó **N.6.1**.

A.7.1
Grégoire, R. 'Repertorium liturgicum Italicum,' *Studi medievali* 3rd ser. 9 (1968) 463-592, with addenda in 11 (1970) 537-56 and 14 (1973) 1123-32.
A.7.2
Olivar, Alejandro. *Els manuscrits litúrgics de la Biblioteca de Montserrat.* Scripta et documenta 18 (Montserrat 1969)
R: *Studia monastica* 11 (1969) 442-7: V. Saxer.
A.7.3
Eizenhöfer, Leo and Hermann Knaus. *Die liturgischen Handschriften der Hessischen Landes- und Hochschulbibliothek Darmstadt* (Wiesbaden 1968)
R: *Bibliothèque de l'école des chartes* 127 (1969) 225-30: M. Huglo.
A.7.4
Leisibach, Josef. *Die liturgischen Handschriften der Kantons- und Universitätsbibliothek Freiburg; ... des Kantons Freiburg (ohne Kantonsbibliothek).* Iter Helveticum, ed. Pascal Ladner, pts. i-ii, = SF Subsidia 15-16 (Fribourg 1976-7)
R: *Speculum* 54 (1979) 392: R.W. Pfaff.
A.7.5
Salmon, Pierre. *Les Manuscrits liturgiques latins de la Bibliothèque Vaticane,* I: *Psautiers, antiphonaires, hymnaires, collectaires, bréviaires.* ST 251 (Rome 1968); II: *Sacramentaires, épistoliers, évangéliaires, graduels, missels.* ST 253 (1969); III: *Ordines romani, pontificaux, rituels, cérémoniaux.* ST 260 (1970); IV: *Les Livres de lectures de l'office. Les Livres de l'office du chapitre. Les Livres d'heures.* ST 267 (1971); V: *Liste complémentaire. Tables générales.* ST 270 (1972)
R: *JTS* n.s. 20 (1969) 653-4: H. Ashworth (I); *Rivista di storia della chiesa in Italia* 24 (1970) 207-11: V. Saxer (I-II); *ibid.* 26 (1971) 186-90: V. Saxer (III-IV).

A.7.6
Frere, Walter H. *Bibliotheca musico-liturgica: A Descriptive Handlist of the Musical and Latin-Liturgical MSS of the Middle Ages Preserved in the Libraries of Great Britain and Ireland.* 2 vols. Plainsong and Medieval Music Society (London 1901-32).

Liturgical Books

Cf. Wordsworth and Littlehales **L.1.5.**

A.8.1
Swete, Henry B. *Church Services and Service-Books before the Reformation.* 3rd ed. (London 1914; 1st ed. 1896)
The discussion of the books treated — breviary, missal, manual, processional, and pontifical — is sometimes over-simplified, but there is much concise, useful information.

A.8.2
Cabrol, Fernand. *Les Livres de la liturgie latine* (Paris 1930). ET as *The Books of the Latin Liturgy* (London and St. Louis 1932).

A.8.3
Sheppard, Lancelot C. *The Liturgical Books.* Twentieth-Century Encyclopedia of Catholicism 109 (New York 1962).

A.8.4
Balboni, D. 'La catalogazione dei libri liturgici,' *EL* 75 (1961) 223-36.

A.8.5
Fiala, V. and W. Irtenkauf. 'Versuch einer liturgischen Nomenklatur' in *Zur Katalogisierung mittelalterlicher und neuerer Handschriften,* ed. Clemens Köttelwesch. Zeitschrift für Bibliothekswesen und Bibliographie, Sonderheft (Frankfurt am Main 1963) 105-37.

Liturgical Latin

A.9.1
Klauser, T. 'Der Übergang der römischen Kirche von der griechischen zur lateinischen Liturgiesprache' in *Miscellanea G. Mercati*, I, ST 121 (Rome 1946) 467-82.
A.9.2
Manz, Georg. *Ausdrucksformen der lateinischen Liturgiesprache bis ins elfte Jahrhundert.* TA Beiheft 1 (Beuron 1950).
A.9.3
Mohrmann, Christine. *Liturgical Latin: Its Origins and Character* (Washington 1957).
A.9.4
Mohrmann, Christine. *Etudes sur le latin des chrétiens*, III: *Latin chrétien et liturgique.* Storia e letteratura 103 (Rome 1965)
R: *RHE* 61 (1966) 354-5: J. Ruysschaert.
A.9.5
Blaise, Albert, with Antoine Dumas. *Le Vocabulaire latin des principaux thèmes liturgiques* (Turnhout 1966)
R: *EL* 81 (1967) 91-2: F. Combaluzier.

Collections of Liturgical Texts

A.10.1
Cabrol, Fernand and Henri Leclercq, eds. *Reliquiae liturgicae vetustissimae.* Monumenta ecclesiae liturgica 1 (Paris 1900-02).
A.10.2
Quasten, Johannes, ed. *Monumenta eucharistica et liturgica vetustissima.* Florilegium patristicum 7 (Bonn 1935-6, in 7 fascicles).
A.10.3
West, Ronald C. *Western Liturgies* (London 1938)
English translations of the Roman, Ambrosian, Gallican, Mozarabic, Celtic, and Sarum eucharistic rites.
A.10.4
Solano, Jesus, ed. *Textos eucaristicos primitivos.* 2 vols. Biblioteca de autores cristianos 88, 118 (Madrid 1952, 1954)
Volume I includes texts (original languages plus Spanish translation) to the

4th century, volume II from the 4th through 6th, with briefer excerpts from the 7th and 8th centuries.

A.10.5

Beckmann, Joachim. *Quellen zur Geschichte des christlichen Gottesdienstes* (Gütersloh 1956)

Pages 1-120 consist of Greek and Latin sources concerning the eucharist through the early middle ages, with German translation of Greek texts.

A.10.6

Hänggi, Anton and Irmgard Pahl. *Prex eucharistica: Textus e variis liturgiis antiquioribus selecti.* SF 12 (Fribourg 1968)

R: *EL* 82 (1968) 247-9: C. Braga.

Early and Eastern Liturgy: Background

Early Liturgy

GENERAL

B.1.1
Palmer, William. *Origines liturgicae.* 2 vols. 2nd ed. (Oxford 1836; 1st ed.
1832) I, 3-197: 'Dissertation on Primitive Liturgies'
Still of value for the information it offers as well as a monument of early
liturgical study.
B.1.2
Duchesne, Louis. *Origines du culte chrétien* (Paris 1889; 3rd ed. 1902; '5th'
ed. 1919). ET of 3rd and '5th' eds. as *Christian Worship: Its Origin and
Evolution* (London 1903 and 1919)
Subtitled 'a study of the Latin liturgy up to the time of Charlemagne,' this
work though somewhat dated is still deservedly a classic. There is an exten-
sive apparatus of texts.
B.1.3
Warren, Frederick E. *The Liturgy and Ritual of the Ante-Nicene Church.*
2nd ed. (London 1912; 1st ed. 1897).
B.1.4
Wordsworth, John. *The Ministry of Grace.* 2nd ed. (London 1903; 1st ed.
1901)
Pages 13-108 and 304-438 are a succinct if somewhat old-fashioned sum-
mary of the early liturgy, considered especially from the standpoint of
those who performed it.
B.1.5
Woolley, Reginald M. *The Liturgy of the Primitive Church* (Cambridge 1910).

B.1.6
Srawley, James H. *The Early History of the Liturgy*. 2nd ed. (Cambridge 1947, considerably revised from 1st ed. 1913).
B.1.7
Lietzmann, Hans. *Messe und Herrenmahl* (Bonn 1926; repr. Berlin 1941, 1955, 1967). ET as *Mass and Lord's Supper* (Leiden 1953-76, in 10 fascicles).
B.1.8
Baumstark, Anton. *Comparative Liturgy*. ET (London 1958) of Bernard Botte's 3rd rev. French ed. (1953) of orig. German ed. of 1939
This knotty and sometimes too speculative work presupposes considerable prior knowledge of the main outlines of liturgical history. The English version is the normative one.
B.1.9
Jungmann, Josef A. *The Early Liturgy to the Time of Gregory the Great* (Notre Dame 1959).
B.1.10
Werner, Eric. *The Sacred Bridge: Liturgical Parallels in Synagogue and Early Church*. Paperback ed. (New York 1970). This is pt. i of a large work of the same title, the rest of which is not here germane (New York 1959).

The *Apostolic Tradition* of (?) Hippolytus and Other Early Church Orders

B.2.1
Dix, Gregory, ed. *The Treatise on the Apostolic Tradition of St.Hippolytus of Rome* (London 1937; reissued with supplement by Henry Chadwick, London 1968).
B.2.2
Hanssens, Jean-Michel. *La Liturgie d'Hippolyte: Ses documents, son titulaire, ses origines, et son caractère.* Orientalia Christiana analecta 155 (Rome 1959).
B.2.3
Botte, Bernard, ed. *La Tradition apostolique de S. Hippolyte: Essai de reconstitution.* LQF 39 (Münster 1963)
R: *Revue des sciences religieuses* 40 (1966) 307-10: H. Chirat.

B.2.4
Hanssens, Jean-Michel. *La Liturgie d'Hippolyte: Documents et études* (Rome 1970)
R: *Bulletin de littérature ecclésiastique* 72 (1971) 300-1: A.-G. Martimort.
B.2.5
Funk, Franz X., ed. *Didascalia et constitutiones apostolorum.* 2 vols. (Paderborn 1905).
B.2.6
Tidner, Erik. *Didascaliae apostolorum, canonum ecclesiasticorum, traditionis apostolicae versiones Latinae.* Texte und Untersuchungen 75 (Berlin 1963)
R: *Bulletin de théologie ancienne et médiévale* 9 (1964) 595: B. Botte.

Post-Nicene Eastern Liturgy

GENERAL

B.3.1
Raes, Alphonsus. *Introductio in liturgiam orientalem* (Rome 1947)
The most scholarly one-volume compendium.
B.3.2
Hanssens, Jean-Michel. *Institutiones liturgicae de ritibus orientalibus,* 'II' [no more appeared]: *De missa rituum orientalium.* 2 vols. plus appendix (Rome 1930-32).
B.3.3
Salaville, Sévérien. *Liturgies orientales* (Paris 1932). ET as *An Introduction to the Study of Eastern Liturgies* (London 1938).
B.3.4
King, Archdale A. *The Rites of Eastern Christendom.* 2 vols. (Rome 1947-8; repr. New York 1972)
This must be used with the caution which is necessary for all of this author's works.
B.3.5
Dalmais, Irénée-Henri. *The Eastern Liturgies.* Twentieth-Century Encyclopedia of Catholicism 111. ET (New York 1960) from French original (Paris 1959)
The simplest introduction.

COLLECTIONS OF LITURGICAL TEXTS

B.4.1

Brightman, Frank E. *Liturgies Eastern and Western*, I: *Eastern Liturgies* (Oxford 1896; repr. 1965). No more published

A reworking of C.E. Hammond, *Liturgies Eastern and Western* (Oxford 1878), with vastly expanded apparatus and minutely detailed scholarship. The four major sections treat the Syrian, Egyptian, Persian (i.e. Nestorian), and Byzantine rites.

B.4.2

Neale, John Mason and R.F. Littledale. *The Liturgies of SS. Mark, James, Clement, Chrysostom, and Basil, and the Church of Malabar, Translated, with Introduction and Appendices.* 2nd ed. (London 1869; 1st ed. 1859) Though more theological than scholarly in approach, this set of translations of five Greek liturgies is still often useful.

Early Liturgy

MISCELLANEOUS

B.5.1

Cabrol, Fernand. *Les Origines liturgiques* (Paris 1906).

B.5.2

Baumstark, A. 'Das Gesetz der Erhaltung des Alten in liturgisch hochwertiger Zeit,' *JLW* 7 (1927) 1-23.

B.5.3

Shepherd, M.H., Jr. 'The Origin of the Church's Liturgy,' *Studia liturgica* 1 (1962) 83-100.

The Mass

General

Cf. Martimort A.2.16.

C.1.1
Jungmann, Josef A. *Missarum sollemnia: Eine genetische Erklärung der römischen Messe.* 6th ed. (Vienna 1966). ET from rev. [= 2nd] German ed. of 1949 as *The Mass of the Roman Rite,* 2 vols. (New York 1951-5) The standard work on the subject; exhaustive, but not easy to use. The abridged one-volume English translation (New York 1955) omits the all-important references.

C.1.2
Fortescue, Adrian. *The Mass: A Study of the Roman Liturgy.* 2nd ed. (London 1913; 1st ed. 1912).

C.1.3
Batiffol, Pierre. *Leçons sur la messe* (Paris 1918).

C.1.4
Cabrol, Fernand. *La Messe en Occident* (Paris 1932). ET as *The Mass of the Western Rites* (London 1934).

Missals

Cf. Ferreres N.3.4.

C.2.1
Ebner, Adalbert. *Quellen und Forschungen zur Geschichte und Kunstgeschichte des* Missale Romanum *im Mittelalter: Iter Italicum* (Freiburg 1896; repr. Graz 1957).
C.2.2
Baudot, Jules. *Le Missel romain: Ses origines, son histoire.* 2 vols. (Paris 1912).
C.2.3
Leroquais, Victor. *Les Sacramentaires et les missels manuscrits des bibliothèques publiques de France.* 3 vols. plus plates (Paris 1924).
C.2.4
Baumstark, Anton. *Missale Romanum: Seine Entwicklung, ihre wichtigsten Urkunden und Probleme* (Eindhoven 1929).
C.2.5
Dold, Alban. *Vom Sakramentar, Comes, und Capitulare zum Missale: Eine Studie über die Entstehungszeit der erstmals vollständig erschlossenen liturgischen Palimpsesttexte in Unziale aus Codex 271 von Monte Cassino.* TA 34 (Beuron 1943).

Ordinary of the Mass

C.3.1
Botte, Bernard and Christine Mohrmann. *L'Ordinaire de la messe: Texte critique, traduction, et études.* Etudes liturgiques 2 (Paris 1953).
C.3.2
Bishop, E. '*Kyrie eleison:* A Liturgical Consultation' in *Liturgica historica* (see A.4.1) 116-36. First publ. 1899-1900.
C.3.3
Capelle, B. 'Le *Kyrie* de la messe et le pape Gélase,' *RB* 46 (1934) 126-44.
C.3.4
Callewaert, C. 'Les Etapes de l'histoire du *Kyrie*,' *RHE* 38 (1942) 20-45.
C.3.5
Molin, J.-B. 'Les Manuscrits de la *Deprecatio Gelasii:* Usage privé des psaumes et dévotion aux litanies,' *EL* 90 (1976) 113-48.

C.3.6
Brinktrine, J. 'Zur Entstehung und Erklärung des *Gloria in excelsis*,'
Römische Quartalschrift 35 (1927) 303-15.
C.3.7
Capelle, B. 'Le Texte du *Gloria in excelsis*,' *RHE* 44 (1949) 439-57.
C.3.8
Capelle, B. 'L'Introduction du symbole à la messe' in *Mélanges Joseph de Ghellinck*, II. Museum Lessianum, sect. hist. 14 (Gembloux 1951) 1003-27.

Mass Formulas (Orations)

C.4.1
Bruylants, Pierre. *Les Oraisons du missel romain.* 2 vols. Etudes liturgiques
1 (Louvain 1952; repr. 1965).
C.4.2
Pflieger, André. *Liturgicae orationis concordantia verbalia*, I: *Missale Romanum* (Rome 1964). No more published
R: *EL* 79 (1965) 78-9: L. Rancati.
C.4.3
Capelle, B. 'Collecta,' *RB* 42 (1930) 197-204.
C.4.4
Jungmann, J.A. '*Oratio super populum* und altchristliche Büssersegnung,'
EL 52 (1938) 77-96.
C.4.5
Eizenhöfer, L. 'Untersuchungen zum Stil und Inhalt der römischen *Oratio super populum*,' *EL* 52 (1938) 258-311.
C.4.6
Brou, L. 'Etude historique sur les oraisons des dimanches après la Pentecôte,'
SE 2 (1949) 123-224.
C.4.7
Ellebracht, Mary Pierre. *Remarks on the Vocabulary of the Ancient Orations in the* Missale Romanum. Latinitas Christianorum primaeva 18 (Nijmegen 1963)
R: *RB* 74 (1964) 347: P. Verbraken.
C.4.8
Strittmatter, A. 'An Unknown "Apology" in Morgan MS. 641,' *Traditio* 4 (1946) 179-96.

Chants of the Mass;
Graduals or Mass Antiphonaries

Cf. section H.8.

C.5.1

Solesmes, Benedictines of, ed. *Le Graduel romain: Edition critique*, II: *Les Sources* (Solesmes 1957); IV: *Le Texte neumatique*, pt. i *Le Groupement des manuscrits* (1960), pt. ii *Les Relations généalogiques des manuscrits* (1962). Vols. I and III not yet published

Important review of II in *Scriptorium* 14 (1960) 80-97: F. de Meeûs, with note by S.J.P. van Dijk, 'Sources of the Roman Gradual,' pp. 98-100.

C.5.2

Marbach, Carl. *Carmina scripturarum, scilicet antiphonas et responsoria ...* (Strasbourg 1907; repr. Hildesheim 1963).

C.5.3

Pietschmann, P. 'Die nicht dem Psalter entnommenen Messgangstücke auf ihre Textgestalt untersucht,' *JLW* 12 (1932) 87-144.

C.5.4

Froger, J. 'Les Chants de la messe aux viiie et ixe siècles,' *Revue grégorienne* 26 (1947) 161-72, 218-28; 27 (1948) 56-62, 98-107; 28 (1949) 58-65, 94-102.

C.5.5

Chavasse, A. 'Les Plus Anciens Types du lectionnaire et de l'antiphonaire romains de la messe,' *RB* 62 (1952) 3-94.

C.5.6

Froger, J. 'L'*Alleluia* dans l'usage romain,' *EL* 62 (1948) 6-48.

C.5.7

Martimort, A.-G. 'Origine et signification de l'*Alleluia* de la messe romaine' in *Kyriakon: Festschrift Johannes Quasten*, ed. P. Granfield and J.A. Jungmann, II (Münster 1970) 811-34.

C.5.8

Jammers, Ewald. *Das Alleluia in der gregorianischen Messe*. LQF 55 (Münster 1973)

R: *Theologische Literaturzeitung* 99 (1974) 384-6: W. Nagel.

Sequences and Mass-Tropes

Cf. Eggen **N.5.4**, Enrique Planchart **H.13.27**, Frere **H.13.7**, and many of the works in **D.7**.

C.6.1
Kehrein, Joseph, ed. *Lateinische Sequenzen des Mittelalters aus Handschriften und Drucken* (Mainz 1873; repr. Hildesheim 1969).
C.6.2
Blume, Clemens and G.M. Dreves, eds., with H.M. Bannister. *Sequentiae ineditae: Liturgische Prosen des Mittelalters.* Analecta hymnica medii aevi 8, 9, 10, 34, 37, 39, 40, 42, 44 (Leipzig 1890-1904).
C.6.3
Blume, Clemens and H.M. Bannister, eds. *Tropi graduales: Tropen des Missale im Mittelalter,* I: *Tropen zum* Ordinarium missae; II: *Tropen zum* Proprium missarum. Analecta hymnica medii aevi 47, 49 (Leipzig 1905, 1906).
C.6.4
Blume, Clemens and H.M. Bannister, eds. *Thesauri hymnologici prosarium: Die Sequenzen des* Thesaurus hymnologicus *H. A. Daniels und anderer Sequenzenausgaben.* Analecta hymnica medii aevi 53-5 (Leipzig 1911-22).
C.6.5
Husmann, Heinrich. *Tropen- und Sequenzenhandschriften.* Répértoire international des sources musicales B.v.1 (Munich and Duisburg 1964)
R: *Revue de musicologie* 51 (1965) 99-102: M. Huglo.
C.6.6
Rönnau, Klaus. *Die Tropen zum* Gloria in excelsis Deo (Wiesbaden 1967)
R: *Revue de musicologie* 53 (1967) 188-9: M. Huglo.
C.6.7
Evans, Paul. *The Early Trope Repertory of Saint Martial de Limoges.* Princeton Studies in Music 2 (Princeton 1970)
R: *Speculum* 48 (1973) 353-5: D.G. Hughes.
C.6.8
Weiss, Günther. *Introitus-Tropen,* I: *Das Repertoire der südfranzösischen Tropare des 10. und 11. Jahrhunderts.* Monumenta monodica medii aevi 3 (Kassel 1970)
R: *Revue de musicologie* 59 (1973) 143-6: M. Huglo.

C.6.9
Jonsson, Ritva, ed. *Tropes du propre de la messe*, I: *Cycle de Noël*. Corpus troporum 1 = Studia Latina Stockholmiensia 21 (Stockholm 1975).
C.6.10
Marcusson, Olof, ed. *Prosules de la messe*, I: *Tropes de l'*Alleluia. Corpus troporum 2 = Studia Latina Stockholmiensia 22 (Stockholm 1976)
R (both the above): *AB* 96 (1978) 237-8: B. de Gaiffier.
C.6.11
Crocker, Richard L. *The Early Medieval Sequence* (Berkeley 1977)
R: *Church History* 48 (1979) 210-11: R.J. Miller.

Canon and Prefaces

C.7.1
Botte, Bernard. *Le Canon de la messe romaine: Edition critique*. Textes et études liturgiques 2 (Louvain 1935).
C.7.2
Eizenhöfer, Leo. *Canon missae Romanae*, pars prior: *Traditio textus;* pars altera: *Textus propinqui*. RED, series minor 1, 7 (Rome 1954, 1966)
R: *EL* 81 (1967) 165: V. Raffa.
C.7.3
Bishop, Edmund. 'On the Early Texts of the Roman Canon' in *Liturgica historica* (see A.4.1) 77-115. First publ. 1903.
C.7.4
Baumstark, A. 'Das *Communicantes* und seine Heiligenliste,' *JLW* 1 (1921) 5-33.
C.7.5
Browe, P. 'Die Elevation in der Messe,' *JLW* 9 (1929) 20-66.
C.7.6
Kennedy, Vincent L. *The Saints of the Canon of the Mass*. Studi d'antichità cristiana 14 (Rome 1938)
Cf. review article by V. Maurice, 'Les Saints du canon de la messe au moyen âge,' *EL* 52 (1938) 353-84.
C.7.7
Eizenhöfer, L. '*Te igitur* und *Communicantes* im römischen Messkanon,' *SE* 8 (1956) 14-75.

C.7.8
Ratcliff, E.C. 'The Institution Narrative of the Roman *Canon missae:* Its Beginnings and Early Background' in *Studia patristica*, II. Texte und Untersuchungen 64 (Berlin 1957) 64-82.
C.7.9
Ratcliff, E.C., with A.H. Couratin, 'The Early Roman *Canon missae*,' *JEH* 20 (1969) 211-24.

Communion Cycle
(*Pater Noster* through Dismissal)

C.8.1
Browe, P. 'Mittelalterliche Kommunionriten,' *JLW* 15 (1935) 23-66.
C.8.2
Borella, P. 'La *Missa* o *Dismissio catechumenorum* nelle liturgie occidentali,' *EL* 53 (1939) 60-110.
C.8.3
Jungmann, J.A. 'Das *Pater Noster* im Kommunionritus' in *Gewordene Liturgie* (see **A.4.4**) 137-64. First publ. 1934.
C.8.4
Eizenhöfer, L. 'Zur *Pater Noster*-Einleitung der römischen Messe,' *ALW* 4.ii (1956) 325-40.

Votive Masses

C.9.1
Amiet, R. 'La Messe *pro unitate ecclesiae*,' *EL* 76 (1962) 296-334.
C.9.2
Gjerløw, L. 'Votive Masses Found in Oslo,' *EL* 84 (1970) 113-28.

Miscellaneous

C.10.1
King, Archdale A. *Eucharistic Reservation in the Western Church* (London 1965)
R: *Speculum* 42 (1967) 535-6: L. Boyle.

C.10.2
Browe, Peter. *Die Verehrung der Eucharistie im Mittelalter* (Munich 1933; repr. Freiburg 1967).

C.10.3
Molin, J.-B. 'L'*Oratio communis fidelium* au moyen âge in Occident du xe au xve siècle' in *Miscellanea liturgica in onore di S.E. il Card. G. Lercaro,* II (Rome 1967) 313-468.

C.10.4
De Clerck, Paul. *La 'Prière universelle' dans les liturgies latines anciennes: Témoignages patristiques et textes liturgiques.* LQF 62 (Münster 1977)
R: *La Maison-Dieu* no. 129 (1977) 148-52: P.-M. Gy (also on Molin **C.10.3**).

The Daily Office

General; Breviaries

Cf. Pinell **G.6.30**, Van Dijk **H.11.10**, Van Dijk and Walker **K.5.3**, Oury **M.1.3**.

D.1.1
Bäumer, Suitbert. *Histoire du bréviaire.* 2 vols. French translation and revision by R. Biron (Paris 1905) of *Geschichte des Breviers* (Freiburg 1895) This massive work owes a good deal to the scholarship of Edmund Bishop as well as of Bäumer. The French version is the standard one.

D.1.2
Batiffol, Pierre. *Histoire du bréviaire romain.* 3rd ed. (Paris 1911). ET as *History of the Roman Breviary* (London 1912). 1st ed. 1893, ET 1898.

D.1.3
Baudot, Jules. *Le Bréviaire romain: Ses origines, son histoire* (Paris 1907). ET as *The Roman Breviary: Its Sources and History* (London 1909) A convenient boiling-down of much of Bäumer, with some reference also to the work of Batiffol.

D.1.4
Molien, A. 'L'Office romain' in *Liturgia* (see **A.2.3**) 555-610.

D.1.5
Leroquais, Victor. *Les Bréviaires manuscrits des bibliothèques publiques de France.* 5 vols. plus plates (Paris 1934).

D.1.6
Jungmann, Josef A. 'Beiträge zur Struktur des Stundengebets' in *Liturgisches Erbe* (see **A.4.5**) 208-64. First publ. 1950-51. ET **A.4.5**, 157-200.

D.1.7
Salmon, Pierre. *L'Office divin.* Lex orandi 27 (Paris 1959). ET as *The Breviary through the Centuries* (Collegeville, Minn. 1962)
This is not a consecutive history but a set of four important essays on major problems in the history of the daily office.
D.1.8
Salmon, P. 'La Prière des heures' in *L'Eglise en prière* (see **A.2.16**) 809-902.
D.1.9
Salmon, Pierre. *L'Office divin au moyen âge.* Lex orandi 43 (Paris 1967)
R: *AB* 87 (1969) 289-91: B. de Gaiffier.
D.1.10
Raffa, V. 'L'ufficio divino del tempo dei Carolingi e il breviario di Innocenzo III confrontati con la liturgia delle ore de Paolo VI,' *EL* 85 (1971) 206-59.

Early Development

Cf. Salmon **D.1.7**, Pinell **G.6.27**.

D.2.1
Callewaert, C. 'De laudibus matutinis' in *Sacris erudiri* (see **A.4.3**) 53-89
Cf. numerous shorter articles in the same collection, e.g. 'De parvis horis Romanis ante regulam S. Benedicti,' pp. 119-26, and 'Vesperae antiquae in officio praesertim Romano,' pp. 91-117.
D.2.2
Dugmore, Clifford W. *The Influence of the Synagogue upon the Divine Office* (Oxford 1944; 2nd ed. publ. as ACC 45, 1964).
D.2.3
Froger, Jacques. *Les Origines de prime.* Bibliotheca 'Ephemerides liturgicae' 19 (Rome 1946).
D.2.4
Jungmann, J.A. 'Die Entstehung des Matutin' in *Liturgisches Erbe* (see **A.4.5**) 139-62. First publ. 1950. ET **A.4.5**, 105-22.
D.2.5
Hanssens, Jean-Michel. *Aux origines de la prière liturgique: Nature et genèse de l'office des matines.* Analecta Gregoriana 57 (Rome 1952).

D.2.6
Jungmann, J.A. 'Die vormonastische Morgenhöre im gallisch-spanischen Raum des 6. Jhts.' in *Liturgisches Erbe* (see **A.4.5**) 163-207. First publ. 1956. ET **A.4.5**, 122-57.
D.2.7
Baumstark, Anton. *Nocturna laus: Typen frühchristlicher Vigilienfeier und ihr Fortleben vor allem in römischen und monastischen Ritus,* ed. Odilo Heiming. LQF 32 (Münster 1957; repr. 1967 with supplements by Heiming).
D.2.8
Winkler, G. 'Über die Kathedralvesper in den verschiedenen Riten des Ostens und Westens,' *ALW* 16 (1974) 53-102.

Monastic Development and Influence

Cf. Pinell **G.6.30**.

D.3.1
Luykx, B. 'L'Influence des moines sur l'office paroissial,' *La Maison-Dieu* no. 51 (1957) 55-81.
D.3.2
Heiming, O. 'Zum monastischen Offizium von Kassianus bis Kolumbanus,' *ALW* 7.1 (1961) 89-156.

Psalter(s), Psalter Collects

Cf. Pinell **G.6.11**.

D.4.1
Leroquais, Victor. *Les Psautiers manuscrits latins des bibliothèques publiques de France.* 2 vols. plus plates (Mâcon 1940-41).
D.4.2
Brou, Louis, ed. *Psalter Collects from v-vi[th] Century Sources, edited from the Papers of André Wilmart.* HBS 83 (London 1949).

D.4.3
Verbraken, (Pierre-)Patrick. *Oraisons sur les cent cinquante psaumes.* Lex orandi 42 (Paris 1967)
R: *EL* 82 (1968) 380-82: A.M. Triacca.
D.4.4
Pascher, J. *Die Methode der Psalmenauswahl im römischen Stundengebet.* Sitzungsberichte der bayerischen Akademie der Wissenschaften, phil.-hist. Klasse, Jahrg. 1967, Heft 3 (Munich 1967) 30 pp.

Collects, Collectars, Office-Blessings

Cf. Dewick **H.13.13**, Unterkircher **H.14.2**, Meersseman **J.1.2**.

D.5.1
Gy, P.-M. 'Collectaire, rituel, processionnal,' *Revue des sciences philosophiques et théologiques* 44 (1960) 441-69.
D.5.2
Heiming, O. 'Das Kollektarfragment des Sangallensis 349, Seiten 5-36' in *Mélanges Botte* (see **A.4.10**) 175-203.
D.5.3
Salmon, Pierre. 'Bénédictions de l'office des matines, nouvelles séries' in his *Analecta liturgica: Extraits des manuscrits liturgiques de la Bibliothèque Vaticane.* ST 273 (Rome 1974) 47-66.

Chants, Antiphonaries

Cf. Marbach **C.5.2**, Jammers **D.9.3**.

D.6.1
Hesbert, Réné-Jean. *Corpus antiphonalium officii,* I: *Manuscripti 'Cursus Romanus';* II: *Manuscripti 'Cursus monasticus';* III: *Invitatoria et antiphonae;* IV: *Responsoria, versus, hymni, et varia;* V: *Fontes earumque prima ordinatio;* VI: *Secunda et tertia ordinationes.* RED, series maior 7-12 (Rome 1963-79) Noteworthy reviews of I, *JTS* n.s. 16 (1965) 239-41: D. Wulstan; I-IV, *Theologisches Revue* 69 (1973) 144-8: H. Becker; V, *Bulletin de littérature ecclésiastique* 77 (1976) 309-13: A.-G. Martimort.

D.6.2
Alfonso, Pio. *I Responsori biblici dell'ufficio romano.* Lateranum, nova series 21 (Rome 1936).

D.6.3
LeRoux, R. 'Aux origines de l'office festif: Les Antiennes et les psaumes de matines et de laudes pour Noël et le Ier Janvier,' *Etudes grégoriennes* 4 (1961) 65-170.

D.6.4
LeRoux, R. 'Etude de l'office dominical et férial: Les Répons *de psalmis* pour les matines de l'Epiphanie à Septuagésime, selon les cursus romain et monastique,' *Etudes grégoriennes* 6 (1963) 39-148.

D.6.5
Claire, J. 'Les Répertoires liturgiques latins avant l'octoéchos, I: L'Office férial romano-franc,' *Etudes grégoriennes* 15 (1975) 5-192.

D.6.6
Franca, Umberto. *Le antifone bibliche dopo Pentecoste: Studio codicologico storico testuale con appendice musicale.* Studia Anselmiana 73 (Rome 1977)
R: *EL* 91 (1977) 522-3: F. Dall'Argento.

Hymns, Hymnaries

Cf. Blume **G.6.10**, Byrnes **K.3.3**.

D.7.1
Chevalier, Ulysse. *Repertorium hymnologicum.* 6 vols. Subsidia hagiographica 4 (Brussels 1892-1921).

D.7.2
Dreves, Guido Maria and Clemens Blume, eds. *Analecta hymnica medii aevi.* 55 vols. (Leipzig 1886-1922) plus 3 vols. Indices (Bern 1978)
Analyzed in Hughes **A.1.3**, 18-19.

D.7.3
Julian, John. *A Dictionary of Hymnology* (London 1892; rev. ed. 1907; repr. New York 1957).

D.7.4
Daniel, Hermann A. *Thesaurus hymnologicus.* 5 vols. in 2 (Leipzig and Halle 1841-56; repr. Hildesheim 1973).

D.7.5

Mone, Franz J. *Lateinische Hymnen des Mittelalters*. 3 vols. (Freiburg 1853-5).

D.7.6

Mearns, James. *Early Latin Hymnaries: An Index of Hymns in Hymnaries before 1100* (Cambridge 1913).

D.7.7

Walpole, A.S. and A.J. Mason. *Early Latin Hymns* (Cambridge 1922; repr. Hildesheim 1966).

D.7.8

Raby, Frederick J.E. *A History of Christian-Latin Poetry from the Beginnings to the Close of the Middle Ages*. 2nd ed. (Oxford 1953; 1st ed. 1927).

D.7.9

Stäblein, Bruno. *Die mittelalterlichen Hymnenmelodien des Abendlandes*. Monumenta monodica medii aevi, Hymnen 1 (Kassel 1956).

D.7.10

Bulst, Walther. *Hymni Latini antiquissimi LXXV. Psalmi III* (Heidelberg 1956).

D.7.11

Connelly, Joseph. *Hymns of the Roman Liturgy* (London 1957).

D.7.12

Vogel, C. 'L'Hymnaire de Murbach contenu dans le manuscrit Junius 25 (Oxford, Bodleian 5137), un témoin du cursus bénédictin ou cursus occidental ancien,' *Archives de l'église d'Alsace* 9 (1958) 1-42
Summary in *EL* 73 (1959) 237-40: F. Combaluzier.

D.7.13

Szövérffy, Josef. *Die Annalen der lateinischen Hymnendichtung*. 2 vols. (Berlin 1964-5)
R: *JTS* n.s. 17 (1966) 496-502: P. Dronke.

D.7.14

Gneuss, Helmut. *Hymnar und Hymnen im englischen Mittelalter: Studien zur Überlieferung, Glossierung, und Übersetzung lateinischer Hymnen in England*. Buchreihe der Anglia 12 (Tübingen 1968)
R: *Speculum* 47 (1972) 759-61: R.H. Robbins.

D.7.15

Szövérffy, Josef. *Iberian Hymnody: Survey and Problems* (Wetteren 1971).
Also publ. in *Classical Folia* 24 (1970) 187-253, 25 (1971) 9-136.

Canticles

Cf. Korhammer **H.13.26.**

D.8.1
Mearns, James. *The Canticles of the Christian Church* (Cambridge 1914).
D.8.2
Schneider, Heinrich. *Die altlateinischen biblischen Cantica.* TA 29/30 (Beuron 1938).

Rhymed, Rhythmical, and Votive Offices

Cf. Ottósson **N.5.9.**

D.9.1
Jonsson, Ritva. *Historia: Etudes sur la genèse des offices versifiés.* Studia Latina Stockholmiensia 15 (Stockholm 1968)
R: *Cahiers de civilisation médiévale* 12 (1969) 183-6: S. Corbin.
D.9.2
Jammers, E. 'Die Antiphonen der rheinischen Reimoffizien,' *EL* 43 (1929) 199-219, 425-51; 44 (1930) 84-99, 342-68.
D.9.3
Jammers, Ewald. *Das Karlsoffizium* Regali natus. Sammlung musikwissenschaftlicher Abhandlung 14 (Leipzig 1934).

Homiliaries

Cf. Barré **H.14.3,** Hosp **H.14.7.**

D.10.1
Grégoire, Réginald. *Les Homéliaires du moyen âge: Inventaire et analyse des manuscrits.* RED, series maior 6 (Rome 1966)
R: *Studia monastica* 19 (1967) 204-7: A. Olivar.
D.10.2
Löw, G. 'Il più antico sermonario di San Pietro in Vaticano,' *Rivista di archeologia cristiana* 19 (1942) 143-83.

D.10.3
Etaix, R. 'Un Homiliaire ancien dans le manuscrit LII de la Bibliothèque
capitulaire de Vérone,' *RB* 73 (1963) 289-306.

D.10.4
Grégoire, R. 'L'Homéliaire romain d'Agimond,' *EL* 82 (1968) 257-305.

D.10.5
Müller, I. 'Lektionar und Homiliar im hochmittelalterlichen Brevier von
Disentis (Cod. Sangall. 403),' *ALW* 11 (1969) 77-164.

D.10.6
Grégoire, R. 'L'Homéliaire de St.-Pierre au Vatican,' *Studi medievali* 3rd
ser. 13 (1972) 233-55.

The Occasional Offices

General

E.1.1
Villien, Antoine. *The History and Liturgy of the Sacraments*. ET (London 1932) of *Les Sacrements, histoire et liturgie* (Paris 1931)*
This hodge-podge of facts and customs from all periods must be used cautiously, but contains a good deal of out-of-the-way information about rites for the occasional offices.
E.1.2
Kingsford, Hugh S., ed. *Illustrations of the Occasional Offices of the Church in the Middle Ages from Contemporary Sources*. ACC 24 (London 1921).
E.1.3
Pascher, Joseph. *Die Liturgie der Sakramente*. 3rd ed. (Münster 1962; 1st ed. 1950).

Rituals (*alias* Manuals)

Cf. Gy D.5.1, Magistretti G.3.11, Hürlimann J.5.12, Maskell L.1.2, Collins L.2.9, Henderson L.3.3, Franz N.1.6, Bragança N.4.5, Faehn N.5.2, Ottosen N.5.8, Kohler N.7.2.

E.2.1
Arx, W. von. 'Zur Entstehungsgeschichte des Rituale,' *Zeitschrift für schweizerische Kirchengeschichte* 63 (1969) 39-57.

E.2.2
Molin, J.-B. 'Pour une bibliographie des rituels,' *EL* 73 (1959) 218-24.
E.2.3
Vanhengel, M.P. 'Le Rite et la formule de la chrismation post-baptismale
en Gaule et en Haute-Italie du ive au viiie siècle d'après les sacramentaires
gallicans: Aux origines du rituel primitif,' *SE* 21 (1972-73) 161-222.

Benedictionals

Cf. Brückmann **E.4.7**, Moeller **E.15.4**, Wilson **H.13.10** and **H.13.12**, Woolley
H.13.14 and **L.1.7**, Amiet **J.1.3**.

E.3.1
Laporte, J. 'Bénédictions épiscopales à Paris (Bibl. nat. lat. 2294, s. x),' *EL*
71 (1957) 145-84.
E.3.2
Rius Serra, J. 'Benediciones episcopales en un manuscrito de Roda,' *HS* 10
(1957) 161-210.
E.3.3
Combaluzier, F. 'Un Bénédictionnaire épiscopal du xe siècle (Ms. 2657
Bibl. Sainte-Geneviève, Paris),' *SE* 14 (1963) 286-342.
E.3.4
Deshusses, J. 'Le Bénédictionnaire gallican du viiie siècle,' *EL* 77 (1963)
169-87.
E.3.5
Moeller, E. 'Le *Liber benedictionum pontificalium* de Guillaume Durand,
évêque de Mende (composé entre 1280 et 1290),' *Questions liturgiques et
paroissiales* 49 (1968) 12-42, 115-36.
E.3.6
Dell' Oro, F. 'Le *Benedictiones episcopales* del codice Warmondiano
(Ivrea, Bibl. cap. 10 XX),' *ALW* 12 (1970) 148-254.

Pontificals

GENERAL

Cf. Magistretti **G.3.9**, Greenwell **H.13.2**, Wilson **H.13.10**, Lindelöf **H.13.15**, Doble **H.13.17**, Turner **H.13.21**; Metzger **H.14.1**, Unterkircher **H.14.2**, Vogel and Elze **J.1.1**, Henderson **L.3.4**, Wordsworth **L.5.6**, and Bragança **N.4.6**.

E.4.1
Andrieu, Michel, ed. *Le Pontifical romain au moyen-âge*, I: *Le Pontifical romain du xii*[e] *siècle;* II: *Le Pontifical de la Curie romaine au xiii*[e] *siècle;* III: *Le Pontifical de Guillaume Durand;* IV: *Tables alphabétiques.* ST 86-8, 99 (Rome 1938-40, 1941).
E.4.2
Frere, Walter H. et al. *Pontifical Services Illustrated from Miniatures of the 15th and 16th Centuries.* 4 vols. ACC 3, 4, 8, 12 (London 1901-8).
E.4.3
Wilson, Henry A., ed. *The Pontifical of Magdalen College.* HBS 39 (London 1910).
E.4.4
De Puniet, Pierre. *Le Pontifical romain: Histoire et commentaire.* 2 vols. (Louvain 1930). ET of vol. I as *The Roman Pontifical* (London 1932).
E.4.5
Leroquais, Victor. *Les Pontificaux manuscrits des bibliothèques publiques de France.* 3 vols. plus plates (Paris 1937).
E.4.6
Amiet, R. 'Un Nouveau Témoin du pontifical romain du xiie siècle,' *Scriptorium* 22 (1968) 231-42.
E.4.7
Brückmann, J. 'Latin Manuscript Pontificals and Benedictionals in England and Wales,' *Traditio* 29 (1973) 391-458.
E.4.8
Amiet, Robert, ed. *Pontificale Augustanum: Le Pontifical du xi*[e] *siècle de la Bibl. capit. d'Aoste (Cod. 15).*Monumenta liturgica ecclesiae Augustanae 3 (Aosta 1975)
R: *Cahiers de civilisation médiévale* 21 (1978) 157-8: R. Grégoire.

Ceremonials

E.5.1

Schimmelpfennig, Bernhard. *Die Zeremonienbücher der römischen Kurie im Mittelalter.* Bibliothek des deutschen historischen Instituts in Rom 40 (Tübingen 1973). Both front cover and spine read 'Kirche' for 'Kurie' R: *English Historical Review* 90 (1975) 164-5: H.S. Offler.

E.5.2

Nabuco, J. 'La Liturgie papale et les origines du Cérémonial des évêques' in *Miscellanea Mohlberg* I (Rome 1948) 283-300.

E.5.3

Tamburini, Filippo, ed., with J. Nabuco. *Le Cérémonial apostolique avant Innocent VIII.* Bibliotheca 'Ephemerides liturgicae' 30 (Rome 1966) R: *EL* 81 (1967) 94-7: P. Borella.

E.5.4

Dykmans, M. 'Le Cérémonial de Grégoire X (vers 1273),' *Gregorianum* 53 (1972) 535-65.

E.5.5

Dykmans, M. 'Le Cérémonial du cardinal-évêque vers 1280,' *Questions liturgiques* 54 (1973) 81-128.

E.5.6

Dykmans, Marc. *Le Cérémonial papal de la fin du moyen âge à la Renaissance, I: Le Cérémonial papal du xiiie siècle.* Bibliothèque de l'Institut historique belge de Rome 24 (Brussels and Rome 1977) R: *Bulletin de littérature ecclésiastique* 80 (1979) 55-7: A.-G. Martimort.

Consecration of Churches

Cf. *DACL* A.2.2, 4.i.374-405.

E.6.1

Stiefenhofer, Dionys. *Die Geschichte der Kirchweihe von ersten bis zum siebsten Jahrhundert.* Veröffentlichungen aus dem kirchenhistorischen Seminar München, 3rd ser. 8 (Munich 1909).

E.6.2

Benz, S. 'Zur Geschichte der römischen Kirchweihe nach den Texten des 6. bis 7. Jahrhunderts' in *Enkainia: Gesammelte Arbeiten zum 800jährigen*

Weihegedächtnis der Abteikirche Maria-Laach, ed. Hilarius Emonds (Düsseldorf 1956) 62-109
See also the essay by Emonds there, 'Enkainia – Weihe und Weihegedächtnis,' pp. 30-57.
E.6.3
Magne, J. 'La Bénédiction d'autel: *Singulare illud repropitiatorium.* Préhistoire et histoire du texte,' *Vigiliae Christianae* 19 (1965) 169-89.
E.6.4
Gros, M.S. 'El ordo romano-hispánico de Narbona para la consagracion de iglesias,' *HS* 19 (1966) 321-401.

Ordination

E.7.1
Andrieu, M. 'Les Ordres mineurs dans l'ancien rit romain,' *Revue des sciences religieuses* 5 (1925) 232-74.
E.7.2
Michels, Thomas. *Beiträge zur Geschichte des Bischofsweihetages im christlichen Altertum und im Mittelalter.* LQF 22 (Münster 1927).
E.7.3
Batiffol, P. 'La Liturgie du sacre des évêques dans son évolution historique,' *RHE* 23 (1927) 733-63.
E.7.4
Snijders, A. '*Acolythus cum ordinatur:* Eine historische Studie,' *SE* 9 (1957) 163-98.
E.7.5
Ellard, Gerald. *Ordination Anointings in the Western Church before 1000 A.D.* Mediaeval Academy of America Publications 16 (Cambridge, Mass. 1933).
E.7.6
Kleinheyer, Bruno. *Die Priesterweihe im römischen Ritus: Eine liturgie-historische Studie.* Trierer theologische Studien 12 (Trier 1962)
R: *JTS* n.s. 15 (1964) 189-91: S.J.P. van Dijk.
E.7.7
Porter, Harry Boone. *The Ordination Prayers of the Ancient Western Churches.* ACC 49 (London 1967)
R: *JEH* 19 (1968) 276: B. Minchin.

E.7.8

Brandolini, L. 'L'evoluzione storica dei riti delle ordinazioni,' *EL* 83 (1969) 67-87.

E.7.9

Richter, Klemens. *Die Ordination des Bischofs von Rom: Eine Untersuchung zur Weiheliturgie.* LQF 60 (Münster 1976)
R: *Theologisches Revue* 73 (1977) 242-4: B. Kleinheyer.

E.7.10

Santantoni, Antonio. *L'ordinazione episcopale: Storia e teologia dei riti dell'ordinazione nelle antiche liturgie dell'Occidente.* Studia Anselmiana 69 (Rome 1976)
R: *EL* 91 (1977) 521-2: R.M. Cervini.

Monastic Profession and Consecration of Virgins

E.8.1

Casel, O. 'Die Mönchsweihe,' *JLW* 5 (1925) 1-47.

E.8.2

Oppenheim, P. 'Mönchsweihe und Taufritus' in *Miscellanea Mohlberg* (see A.4.7) I, 259-82.

E.8.3

Frank, H. 'Untersuchungen zur Geschichte der benediktinischen Profess-liturgie im frühen Mittelalter,' *Studien und Mitteilungen zur Geschichte des Benediktiner-ordens und seiner Zweige* 63 (1951) 93-139.

E.8.4

Hofmeister, P. 'Benediktinische Professriten,' *Studien und Mitteilungen zur Geschichte des Benediktiner-ordens und seiner Zweige* 74 (1963) 241-85.

E.8.5

Gräf, H.J. '*Ad monachum faciendum:* Die Mönchsprofess nach einem Fest-Sakramentar von Venedig aus dem xi. Jht.,' *EL* 88 (1974) 353-69.

E.8.6

Metz, René. *La Consécration des vierges dans l'église romaine: Etude d'histoire de la liturgie.* Bibliothèque de l'Institut de droit canonique de l'Université de Strasbourg 4 (Paris 1954).

E.8.7

Metz, R. 'Benedictio sive consecratio virginum?' *EL* 80 (1966) 265-93.

Baptism

Cf. *DACL* **A**.2.2, 2.i.251-346; Schmidt **A**.2.14, 238-321; Martimort **A**.2.16, 528-84; Duchesne **B**.1.2, ET 292-341; Thompson **E**.10.1, Akeley **G**.6.31, Nocent **M**.2.8.

E.9.1
Whitaker, Edward C. *Documents of the Baptismal Liturgy.* ACC 42 (London 1960; 2nd ed. 1970)
R: *JEH* 12 (1961) 261: R.C.D. Jasper
English translations of excerpts from some forty sources for the history of the baptismal rite, from the ante-Nicene period to the early middle ages.
E.9.2
Fisher, John D.C. *Christian Initiation: Baptism in the Medieval West.* ACC 47 (London 1965)
R: *JTS* n.s. 17 (1966) 494-6: J.H. Crehan.
E.9.3
Dondeyne, A. 'La Discipline des scrutins dans l'église latine avant Charlemagne,' *RHE* 28 (1932) 1-33, 751-87.
E.9.4
Scheidt, Hubert. *Die Taufwasserweihgebete: Im Sinne vergleichender Liturgieforschung untersucht.* LQF 29 (Münster 1935).
E.9.5
Stenzel, Alois. *Die Taufe: Eine genetische Erklärung der Taufliturgie.*
Forschungen zur Geschichte der Theologie und des innerkirchlichen Lebens 7-8 (Innsbruck 1958)
Cf. review article by J.M. Hanssens, 'Scrutins et sacramentaires,' *Gregorianum* 41 (1960) 692-700.
E.9.6
Olivar, A. 'Vom Ursprung der römischen Taufwasserweihe,' *ALW* 6.1 (1959) 62-78.
E.9.7
Chavasse, A. 'La Discipline romaine des sept scrutins pré-baptismaux,' *Recherches de science religieuse* 48 (1960) 227-40.
E.9.8
De Jong, J.P. '*Benedictio fontis:* Eine genetische Erklärung der römischen Taufwasserweihe,' *ALW* 8.1 (1963) 21-46.

E.9.9
Coebergh, C. 'Problèmes de l'évolution historique et de la structure littéraire de la *benedictio fontis* du rit romain,' *SE* 16 (1965) 260-319.
E.9.10
Mitchell, Leonel L. *Baptismal Anointing.* ACC 48 (London 1966)
R: *JTS* n.s. 18 (1967) 488-90: J.H. Crehan
The period covered is from apostolic times through the early middle ages.
E.9.11
Spital, Hermann J. *Der Taufritus in den deutschen Ritualien von den ersten Drucken bis zur Einführung des* Rituale Romanum. LQF 47 (Münster 1968)
R: *JTS* n.s. 20 (1969) 346-7: J.H. Crehan
The period covered is from roughly 1480 to 1640.

Confirmation

Cf. *DACL* **A.2.2**, 3.ii.2515-44; Vanhengel **E.2.3**.

E.10.1
Thompson, Tom. *The Offices of Baptism and Confirmation* (Cambridge 1914).
E.10.2
Llopart, E. 'Les fórmules de la confirmació en el pontifical romà' in *Liturgica*, II. Scripta et documenta 10 (Montserrat 1958) 121-80.
E.10.3
Lewandowski, B. 'Evolutio ritus liturgiae confirmationis in ecclesia hispanica,' *EL* 85 (1971) 97-120; '... in ecclesia Mediolanensi,' *ibid.* 29-47.
E.10.4
Riggio, G. 'Liturgia e pastorale della confermazione nei secoli xi-xii-xiii,' *EL* 87 (1973) 445-72, 88 (1974) 3-31.
E.10.5
Angenendt, A. 'Bonifatius und das *Sacramentum initiationis:* Zugleich ein Beitrag zur Geschichte der Firmung,' *Römische Quartalschrift* 72 (1977) 133-83.

Marriage

E.11.1
Ritzer, Korbinian. *Formen, Riten, und religiöses Brauchtum der Eheschlies-
sung in den christlichen Kirchen des ersten Jahrtausends.* LQF 38 (Münster
1962). French translation as *Le Mariage dans les églises chrétiennes du i^er
au xie siècle* (Paris 1970)
R: *JTS* n.s.14 (1963) 172-6: W. Ullmann.
E.11.2
Molin, Jean-Baptiste and Protais Mutembe. *Le Rituel du mariage en France
du xiie au xvie siècle.* Théologie historique 26 (Paris 1974)
R: *Studi medievali* 3rd ser. 19 (1978) 527-9: G. Barone.

Penance

E.12.1
Jungmann, Josef A. *Die lateinischen Bussriten in ihrer geschichtlichen
Entwicklung.* Forschungen zur Geschichte des innerkirchlichen Lebens 3-4
(Innsbruck 1932).
E.12.2
Schmitz, Hermann J. *Die Bussbücher und die Bussdisziplin der Kirche*
(Mainz 1883; repr. Graz 1958) esp. pp. 63-102.
E.12.3
Dold, A. 'Eine alte Bussliturgie aus Cod. Vat. lat. 1339,' *JLW* 11 (1931)
94-130.
E.12.4
Gy, P.-M. 'Histoire liturgique du sacrement de pénitence,' *La Maison-Dieu*
no. 56 (1958) 5-21.

Unction

E.13.1
De Clercq, C. '*Ordines unctionis infirmi* des ixe et xe siècles,' *EL* 44 (1930)
100-22.

E.13.2

Browe, P. 'Die letzte Ölung in der abendländischen Kirche des Mittelalters,' *ZKT* 55 (1931) 515-61.

E.13.3

Porter, H.B. 'The Origin of the Medieval Rite for Anointing the Sick or Dying,' *JTS* n.s. 7 (1956) 211-25.

E.13.4

Porter, H.B. 'The Rites for the Dying in the Early Middle Ages, i: St. Theodulf of Orleans; ii: The Legendary Sacramentary of Rheims,' *JTS* n.s. 10 (1959) 43-62, 299-307.

E.13.5

Murray, P. 'The Liturgical History of Extreme Unction' in *Studies in Pastoral Liturgy* II, ed. Vincent Ryan (Dublin 1963) 18-35.

E.13.6

Triacca, A.M. 'Per una rassegna sul sacramento dell'unzione degli infermi,' *EL* 89 (1975) 397-468

The notes, on pages 409-67, amount to a classified bibliography.

Burial

E.14.1

Freistedt, Emil. *Altchristliche Totengedächtnistage und ihre Beziehung zum Jenseitsglauben und Totenkultus der Antike.* LQF 24 (Münster 1928).

E.14.2

Capelle, B. 'L'Antienne *In paradisum*' in his *Travaux liturgiques,* III (Louvain 1967) 252-67. First publ. 1923.

E.14.3

Gougaud, L. 'Etude sur les *Ordines commendationis animae*,' *EL* 49 (1935) 3-27.

E.14.4

Browe, P. 'Die Sterbekommunion im Altertum und Mittelalter,' *ZKT* 60 (1936) 1-54, 211-40.

E.14.5

Callewaert, C. 'De officio defunctorum' in *Sacris erudiri* (see A.4.3) 169-77.

E.14.6
Wilmart, A. 'Un Office monastique pour le 2 novembre dans le nord de la France au xie siècle,' (ed. L. Brou) *SE* 5 (1953) 247-330.
E.14.7
Gay, C. 'Formulaires anciens pour la messe des défunts,' *Etudes grégoriennes* 2 (1957) 83-129.
E.14.8
Frank, H. 'Der älteste erhaltene *Ordo defunctorum* der römischen Liturgie und sein Fortleben in Totenagenden des frühen Mittelalters,' *ALW* 7.2 (1962) 360-415.
E.14.9
Ntedika, Joseph. *L'Evocation de l'au-delà dans la prière pour les morts: Etude de patristique et de liturgie latines (ive-viiie siècles).* Recherches africaines de théologie 2 (Louvain 1971)
R: *EL* 86 (1972) 309-11: A. Pistoia.
E.14.10
Rowell, Geoffrey. *The Liturgy of Christian Burial: An Introductory Survey of the Historical Development of Christian Burial Rites.* ACC 59 (London 1977).

Blessings and Exorcism

E.15.1
Bartsch, Elmar. *Die Sachbeschwörungen der römischen Liturgie.* LQF 46 (Münster 1967)
R: *JTS* n.s. 19 (1968) 345-6: J.H. Crehan.
E.15.2
Franz, Adolph. *Die kirchlichen Benediktionen im Mittelalter.* 2 vols. (Freiburg 1909; repr. Graz 1960).
E.15.3
De Puniet, P. 'Le Pouvoir sacerdotal de bénir,' *EL* 42 (1928) 425-39.
E.15.4
Moeller, Edmond (Eugène), ed. *Corpus benedictionum pontificalium.* 3 vols. Corpus Christianorum, series Latina 162, 162A, 162B (Turnhout 1971-3)
R: *Scriptorium* 32 (1978) 285-6: L. Bieler.

Liturgical Year
and Observances

General

Cf. Dix **A.2.7**, 303-96.

F.1.1
Kellner, K.A.Heinrich. *Heortology: A History of the Christian Festivals from their Origin to the Present Day.* ET (London 1908) of 2nd German ed. (Freiburg 1906).
F.1.2
Dowden, John. *The Church Year and Calendar* (Cambridge 1910).
F.1.3
McArthur, A[lexander] Allan. *The Evolution of the Christian Year* (London 1953).
F.1.4
Pascher, Josef. *Das liturgische Jahr* (Munich 1963)
R: *EL* 78 (1964) 528-30: V. Raffa.

Calendars

Cf. Hennig **F.17.6**, Wormald **H.13.16** and **L.7.14**, Munding **J.5.9**.

F.2.1
Nilles, Nicolaus. *Kalendarium manuale utriusque ecclesiae orientalis et occidentalis.* 2 vols. (Innsbruck 1896-7).

F.2.2
Holweck, Frederick G. *Calendarium liturgicum festorum Dei et Dei matris Mariae* (Philadelphia 1925).
F.2.3
Frere, Walter H. *Studies in Early Roman Liturgy,* I: *The Calendar.* ACC 28 (London 1930).
F.2.4
Loew (Lowe), Elias A. *Die ältesten Kalendarien aus Monte Cassino.* Quellen und Untersuchungen zur lateinischen Philologie des Mittelalters 3, pt. iii (Munich 1908).
F.2.5
Mallardo, Domenico. *Il calendario marmoreo di Napoli.* Bibliotheca 'Ephemerides liturgicae' 18 (Rome 1947).
F.2.6
Hennig, J. 'Kalendar und Martyrologium als Literaturformen,' *ALW* 7.1 (1961) 1-44.

Sunday

F.3.1
Rordorf, Willi. *Der Sonntag: Geschichte des Ruhe- und Gottesdiensttages im ältesten Christentum.* Abhandlungen zur Theologie des alten und neuen Testaments 43 (Zürich 1962). ET (London 1968)
R (of ET): *JEH* 20 (1969) 315-16: R.C.D. Jasper.
F.3.2
Callewaert, C. 'La Synaxe eucharistique à Jérusalem, berceau du dimanche' in *Sacris erudiri* (see **A.4.3**) 263-303.

Advent to Epiphany
(including Christmastide)

Cf. LeRoux **D.6.3**, Rovalo **G.6.29**.

F.4.1
Botte, Bernard. *Les Origines de la Noël et de l'Epiphanie.* Textes et études liturgiques 1 (Louvain 1932).

F.4.2
Jungmann, J.A. 'Advent und Voradvent: Überreste des gallischen Advents in der römischen Liturgie' in *Gewordene Liturgie* (see A.4.4) 232-94. First publ. 1937.
F.4.3
Croce, W. 'Die Adventmessen des römischen Missale in ihrer geschichtlichen Entwicklung,' *ZKT* 74 (1952) 277-317; and 'Die Adventsliturgie im Licht ihrer geschichtlichen Entwicklung,' *ZKT* 76 (1954) 257-96, 440-72.
F.4.4
Maertens, Th. 'L'Avent,' *Mélanges de science religieuse* 18 (1961) 47-110.
F.4.5
Leclercq, J. 'Aux origines du cycle de Noël,' *EL* 60 (1946) 7-26.
F.4.6
Cullmann, Oscar. *Der Ursprung des Weihnachtfestes.* 2nd ed. (Zürich 1960). 1st ed., titled *Weihnachten in der alten Kirche* (Basel 1947), translated as 'The Origin of Christmas' in his *The Early Church* (London 1956) 17-36.
F.4.7
Frank, H. 'Frühgeschichte und Ursprung des römischen Weihnachtsfestes im Lichte neuerer Forschung,' *ALW* 2 (1952) 1-24; revises his 'Zur Geschichte von Weihnachten und Epiphanie,' *JLW* 12 (1932) 145-55 and 13 (1933) 1-38.
F.4.8
Engberding, H. 'Der 25. Dezember als Tag der Feier der Geburt des Herrn,' *ALW* 2 (1952) 25-43.
F.4.9
Lemarié, Joseph. *La Manifestation du Seigneur: La Liturgie de Noël et de l'Epiphanie.* Lex orandi 23 (Paris 1957).
F.4.10
Nikolasch, F. 'Zur Ursprung des Epiphaniefestes,' *EL* 82 (1968) 393-429.

Lent (and Pre-Lent)

F.5.1
Thurston, Herbert. *Lent and Holy Week* (London 1904).
F.5.2
Andrieu, M. 'Les Messes des jeudis de carême et les anciens sacramentaires,' *Revue des sciences religieuses* 9 (1929) 343-75.

F.5.3
Callewaert, C. 'La Durée et le caractère du carême ancien dans l'église latine' in *Sacris erudiri* (see A.4.3) 449-506
Callewaert's many articles on the subject are gathered up in this collection, pages 449-671.
F.5.4
Chavasse, A. 'Le Carême romain et les scrutins prébaptismaux avant le ixe siècle,' *Recherches de science religieuse* 35 (1948) 325-81.
F.5.5
Chavasse, A. 'La Structure du carême et les lectures des messes quadragésimales dans la liturgie romaine,' *La Maison-Dieu* no. 31 (1952) 76-119.
F.5.6
Jungmann, J. 'Die *Quadragesima* in den Forschungen von Antoine Chavasse,' *ALW* 5.1 (1957) 84-95.

Passiontide and Holy Week

Cf. Braun N.7.3.

F.6.1
Tyrer, John W. *Historical Survey of Holy Week, its Services and Ceremonial.* ACC 29 (London 1932).
F.6.2
Wilmart, A. 'L'Hymne de la charité pour le Jeudi-Saint' in his *Auteurs spirituels et textes dévots du moyen-âge latin* (Paris 1932) 26-36.
F.6.3
Rosketh, Y. 'La Liturgie de la Passion vers la fin du xe siècle,' *Revue de musicologie* 28 (1949) 1-58, 29 (1950) 35-52.
F.6.4
Schäfer, Thomas. *Die Fusswaschung im monastischen Brauchtum und in der lateinischen Liturgie: Liturgiegeschichtliche Untersuchung.* TA 47 (Beuron 1956).
F.6.5
Kantorowicz, E. 'The Baptism of the Apostles,' *Dumbarton Oaks Papers* 9/10 (1956) 203-51.
F.6.6
Schmidt, Herman A.P., ed. *Hebdomada Sancta.* 2 vols. (Rome 1956-7).

F.6.7
Gräf, Hermann J. *Palmenweihe und Palmenprozession in der lateinischen Liturgie* (Kaldenkirchen 1959).
F.6.8
Balboni, D. 'Il rito della benedizione delle palme (Vat. lat. 4770)' in *Collectanea Vaticana in honorem Anselmi M. Card. Albareda*, I. ST 219 (Rome 1962) 55-74.

Good Friday

Cf. Gjerløw N.5.10.

F.7.1
Baumstark, A. 'Die Orient und die Gesänge der *Adoratio crucis*,' *JLW* 2 (1922) 1-17.
F.7.2
Willis, Geoffrey G. 'The Solemn Prayers of Good Friday' in his *Essays in Early Roman Liturgy*. ACC 46 (London 1964) 1-48.
F.7.3
Drumbl, J. 'Die Improperien in der lateinischen Liturgie,' *ALW* 15 (1973) 68-100.

Easter

Cf. Dolan F.20.7, Berger F.20.8.

F.8.1
Fischer, Balthazar and J. Wagner, eds. *Paschatis sollemnia: Studien zu Osterfeier und Osterfrömmigkeit. Festschrift J. A. Jungmann* (Basel 1959).
F.8.2
Van der Veken, B.J. 'De primordiis liturgiae Paschalis,' *SE* 13 (1962) 461-501.
F.8.3
Lang, A.P. 'Anklänge an Orationen der Ostervigil in Sermonen Leos des Grossen,' *SE* 13 (1962) 281-325, 18 (1967-8) 5-119.

F.8.4
Frank, H. 'Die Paschavigil als Ende der Quadragesima und ihr Festinhalt bei Augustinus,' *ALW* 9.1 (1965) 1-27.
F.8.5
Avery, Myrtilla. *The* Exultet *Rolls of South Italy*, 2 vols. (Princeton 1936).
F.8.6
Capelle, B. 'L'*Exultet* pascal oeuvre de S. Ambroise' in *Miscellanea G. Mercati*, I. ST 121 (Rome 1946) 219-46.
F.8.7
Fischer, B. 'Ambrosius der Verfasser des österlichen *Exultet?*' *ALW* 2 (1952) 61-74.
F.8.8
Benoît-Castelli, G. 'Le *Praeconium paschale*,' *EL* 67 (1953) 309-34.
F.8.9
Pinell, J.M. 'La benedicció del Ciri pasqual i els seus textos' in *Liturgica*, II. Scripta et documenta 10 (Montserrat 1958) 1-119.
F.8.10
Eizenhöfer, L. 'Die Feier der Ostervigil in der Benediktinerabtei San Silvestro zu Foligno um das Jahr 1100,' *ALW* 6.2 (1960) 339-71.
F.8.11
Fischer, B. 'Die Lesungen der römischen Ostervigil unter Gregor dem Grossen' in *Colligere fragmenta* (see **A.4.8**) 144-59.
F.8.12
Bernal, J.R. 'Los sistemas de lecturas y oraciones en la vigilia pascual hispana,' *HS* 17 (1964) 283-347.

Pentecost and Sundays Following
(including Trinity)

F.9.1
Jungmann, J. 'Pfingstoktav und Kirchenbusse in der römischen Liturgie' in *Miscellanea Mohlberg* (see **A.4.7**) I, 169-82.
F.9.2
Schmidt, H.A.P. 'Die Sonntage nach Pfingsten in den römischen Sakramentaren' in *Miscellanea Mohlberg* (see **A.4.7**) I, 451-93.
F.9.3
Kretschmar, G. 'Himmelfahrt und Pfingsten,' *Zeitschrift für Kirchengeschichte* 66 (1954-5) 209-53.

F.9.4
Cabié, Robert. *La Pentecôte: L'Evolution de la cinquantaine pascale au cours de cinq premiers siècles* (Tournai 1965)
R: *RB* 76 (1966) 370: P. Verbraken.
F.9.5
* Klaus, A. *Ursprung und Verbreitung der Dreifaltigkeitsmesse* (Werl 1938).
F.9.6
Browe, P. 'Zur Geschichte des Dreifaltigkeitsfestes,' *ALW* 1 (1950) 65-81.

Ember Days and Rogation Days

F.10.1
Fischer, Ludwig. *Die kirchlichen Quatember: Ihre Entstehung, Entwicklung, und Bedeutung in liturgischer, rechtlicher, und kulturhistorischer Hinsicht* (Munich 1914).
F.10.2
Willis, G.G. 'Ember Days' in *Essays* (see **F.7.2**) 49-97.
F.10.3
De Bruyne, D. 'L'Origine des processions de la chandeleur et des rogations à propos d'un sermon inédit,' *RB* 34 (1922) 14-26.
F.10.4
* Colette, Marie-Noëlle. *Le Répertoire des rogations d'après un processional de Poitiers, xvie siècle* (Paris 1976)
R: *Etudes grégoriennes* 17 (1978) 234-5: J. Hourlier and J. Claire.

Corpus Christi

F.11.1
Browe, P. 'Die Ausbreitung des Fronleichnamsfestes,' *JLW* 8 (1928) 107-43.
F.11.2
* Browe, Peter. *Textus antiqui de festo Corporis Christi* (Münster 1934).
F.11.3
Lambot, Cyrille and I. Fransen. *L'Office de la Fête-Dieu primitive: Textes et mélodies retrouvés* (Maredsous 1946).
F.11.4
Delaissé, L.M.J. 'A la recherche des origines de l'office du Corpus Christi dans les manuscrits liturgiques,' *Scriptorium* 4 (1950) 220-39.

F.11.5
Matern, Gerhard. *Zur Vorgeschichte und Geschichte der Fronleichnamsfeier besonders in Spanien.* Spanische Forschungen der Görresgesellschaft, 2. Reihe, 10 (Münster 1962)
R: *RHE* 58 (1963) 964-5: G.M. Colombàs.
F.11.6
Cottiaux, J. 'L'Office liégeios de la Fête-Dieu, sa valeur et son destin,'
RHE 58 (1963) 5-81, 405-59.

Miscellaneous Feasts

F.12.1
Hesbert, R.-J. 'Les Trentains grégoriens sous forme de cycles liturgiques,'
RB 81 (1971) 108-22.
F.12.2
Pfaff, R.W. 'The English Devotion of St. Gregory's Trental,' *Speculum* 49
(1974) 75-90.

Liturgies for Individual Saints

Cf. Hohler **L.7.11.**

F.13.1
Hohler, C. 'A Note on *Jacobus,*' *Journal of the Warburg and Courtauld Institutes* 35 (1972) 31-80.
F.13.2
Saxer, Victor. *Le Culte de Marie Madeleine en Occident des origines à la fin du moyen âge.* 2 vols. Cahiers d'archéologie et d'histoire 3 (Auxerre 1959).
F.13.3
Oury, G. 'Les Messes de Saint Martin dans les sacramentaires gallicans, romano-francs, et milanais,' *Etudes grégoriennes* 5 (1962) 73-97; and 'Formulaires anciens pour la messe de Saint Martin,' *ibid.* 7 (1967) 21-40.
F.13.4
Lemarié, J. 'Textes relatifs au culte de l'Archange et des anges dans les bréviaires manuscrits du Mont St. Michel,' *SE* 13 (1962) 113-52; and 'Textes liturgiques concernant le culte de S. Michel,' *SE* 14 (1963) 277-85.

F.13.5
Jones, Charles W. *The St. Nicholas Liturgy and its Literary Relationships, Ninth-Twelfth Centuries.* University of California Publications, English Studies 27 (Berkeley 1963)
See also the review article by Christopher Hohler, *Medium Ævum* 36 (1967) 40-48.
F.13.6
Lietzmann, Hans. *Petrus und Paulus in Rom: Liturgische und archäologische Studien.* Arbeiten zur Kirchengeschichte 1 (Berlin 1927).
F.13.7
Saxer, V. 'Le Culte des apôtres Pierre et Paul dans les plus vieux formulaires romains de la messe du 29 juin: Recherches sur la thématique des sections xv-xvi du sacramentaire Léonien' in *Saecularia Petri et Pauli.* Studi di antichità cristiana 28 (Rome 1969) 199-240.
F.13.8
Stevens, D. 'Music in Honor of St. Thomas of Canterbury,' *Musical Quarterly* 56 (1970) 311-48.

Marian Feasts

Cf. De Bruyne **F.10.3.**

F.14.1
Polc, Jaroslaus V. *De origine festi visitationis B. M. V.* Corona Lateranensis 9A (Rome 1967)
R: *RHE* 64 (1969) 677: P. de Vooght.
F.14.2
Bishop, E. 'On the Origins of the Feast of the Conception of the Blessed Virgin Mary' in *Liturgica historica* (see **A.4.1**) 238-59.
F.14.3
Van Dijk, S.J.P. 'The Origin of the Latin Feast of the Conception of the Blessed Virgin Mary,' *Dublin Review* 118 (1954) 251-67 and 428-42.
F.14.4
Capelle, B. 'La Fête de l'Assomption dans l'histoire liturgique,' *Ephemerides theologicae Lovanienses* 3 (1926) 33-45.
F.14.5
Capelle, B. 'La Fête de la Vierge à Jérusalem au ve siècle,' *Le Muséon* 56 (1943) 1-33.

F.14.6
Deug-Su, I. 'La festa della purificazione in Occidente (secoli vi-viii),' *Studi medievali* 3rd ser. 15 (1974) 143-216.
F.14.7
Jugie, M. 'La première fête mariale en Orient et en Occident: L'Avent primitif,' *Echos d'Orient* 22 (1923) 129-52.
F.14.8
Scheer, A. 'Aux origines de la fête de l'Annonciation,' *Questions liturgiques* 58 (1977) 97-169.

Little Office of the Blessed Virgin Mary; *Horae* and Prymers

Cf. Maskell **L.1.2**, Wordsworth **L.3.5**.

F.15.1
Bishop, E. 'On the Origin of the Prymer' in *Liturgica historica* (see **A.4.1**) 211-37. First publ. 1895, as intro. to H. Littlehales' ed. of *The Prymer or Lay Folks' Prayer Book,* Early English Text Society 109 (1897).
F.15.2
Dewick, E.S., ed. *Facsimiles of* Horae de beata Maria virgine *from English Manuscripts of the Eleventh Century.* HBS 21 (London 1902).
F.15.3
Leroquais, Victor. *Les Livres d'heures manuscrits de la Bibliothèque nationale.* 2 vols. plus plates and supplement (Paris 1927-43).
F.15.4
Leclercq, J. 'Formes successives de l'office votif de la Vierge,' *EL* 72 (1958) 294-301; and 'Formes anciennes de l'office marial,' *EL* 74 (1960) 89-102.
F.15.5
Canal, J.M. 'El oficio parvo de la Virgen de 1000 a 1250,' *Ephemerides Mariologicae* 15 (1965) 463-75.

Other Marian Devotions

F.16.1
Frénaud, G. 'Le Culte de Notre Dame dans l'ancienne liturgie latine' in
Maria, ed. H. du Manoir, VI (Paris 1961) 157-211.
F.16.2
Barré, Henri. *Prières anciennes de l'Occident à la mère du Sauveur, des
origines à S. Anselme* (Paris 1963)
R: *Cahiers de civilisation médiévale* 8 (1965) 201-3: M.-M. Davy.
F.16.3
Canal, J.M. 'Elementos marianos en la antigua liturgia romana,' *Ephemerides
Mariologicae* 16 (1966) 289-317.
F.16.4
Meersseman, Gilles G. *Der* Hymnos akathistos *im Abendland.* 2 vols. SF
2-3 (Fribourg 1958-60).

Martyrologies

Cf. Hennig **F.2.6.**

F.17.1
Quentin, Henri. *Les Martyrologes historiques du moyen âge* (Paris 1908).
F.17.2
Quentin, Henri and H. Delehaye, eds. 'Martyrologium Hieronymianum' in
Acta sanctorum Novembris II. ii (Brussels 1931)
This, with Delehaye's magnificent 'Commentarius perpetuus in Mart.
Hieron.', supplants the edition by G.B. de Rossi and L. Duchesne, *ibid.*
Nov. II. i (1894).
F.17.3
Dubois, Jacques, ed. *Le Martyrologe d'Usuard: Texte et commentaire.*
Subsidia hagiographica 40 (Brussels 1965)
R: *RHE* 61 (1966) 853-6: N. Huyghebaert.
F.17.4
Dubois, Jacques and G. Rénaud, eds. *Edition pratique des martyrologes de
Bède, de l'Anonyme lyonnais, et de Florus* (Paris 1976)
R: *Studia monastica* 19 (1977) 415-16: A. Olivar.

F.17.5
O'Connell, Joseph B., tr. *The Roman Martyrology* (London 1962)
A translation of the *Martyrologium Romanum* of 1956, itself based on that
of 1584 and, ultimately, on Usuard's.
F.17.6
Hennig, J. '*Martyrologium* und *Kalendarium*' in *Studia patristica*, V. Texte
und Untersuchungen 80 (Berlin 1962) 69-82.
F.17.7
De Gaiffier, B. 'De l'usage et de la lecture du martyrologe: Témoignages
antérieurs au xie siècle,' *AB* 79 (1961) 40-59.
F.17.8
De Gaiffier, B. 'La Lecture des passions des martyrs à Rome avant le ixe
siècle,' *AB* 87 (1969) 63-78.
F.17.9
Dubois, J. 'A la recherche de l'état primitif du martyrologe d'Usuard,' *AB*
95 (1977) 43-71.

Processions and Processionals

Cf. Gy **D.5.1**, De Bruyne **F.10.3**, Colette **F.10.4**, Henderson **L.2.5** and
L.3.3, Benoît-Castelli **L.7.5**.

F.18.1
Lengeling, E.J. 'Die Bittprozessionen des Domkapitels und der Pfarreien der
Stadt Münster vor dem Fest Christi Himmelfahrt' in *Monasterium*, ed. A.
Schröer (Münster 1966) 151-220.
F.18.2
Allworth, C. 'The Medieval Processional: Donaueschingen MS. 882,' *EL* 84
(1970) 169-86.
F.18.3
Bailey, Terence. *The Processions of Sarum and the Western Church*. Studies
and Texts 21 (Toronto 1971)
R: *Cahiers de civilisation médiévale* 16 (1973) 59-61: M. Huglo.

Liturgical Expositions;
Allegorization of Liturgy

Cf. Simmons L.3.6.

F.19.1
Wilmart, A. 'Expositio missae,' *DACL* 5.i (1922) 1014-27.

F.19.2
Amalarius of Metz: Hanssens, Jean-Michel, ed. *Amalarii episcopi opera liturgica omnia.* 3 vols. ST 138-40 (Rome 1948-50)
This edition is one of the high-water marks of liturgical scholarship in this century.

F.19.3
Florus of Lyons: Hanssens, J.-M. 'De Flori Lugdunensis "opusculis contra Amalarium",' *EL* 47 (1933) 15-31.

F.19.4
Duc, Paul. *Etude sur l'*Expositio missae *de Florus de Lyon, suivie d'une édition critique du texte* (Belley 1937).

F.19.5
Walafrid Strabo: Hrbata, J. 'De expositione missae Walafridi Strabonis,' *EL* 63 (1949) 145-65.

F.19.6
Bernold of Constance: *Micrologus.* PL 151.974-1022.

F.19.7
Kennedy, V.L. 'For a New Edition of the *Micrologus* of Bernold of Constance' in *Mélanges Andrieu* (see **A.4.9**) 229-41.

F.19.8
Honorius Augustodunensis: *Gemma animae.* PL 172.541-738.

F.19.9
Rupert of Deutz: Haacke, Hrabanus, ed. *Ruperti Tuitensis liber de divinis officiis.* Corpus Christianorum, continuatio medievalis 7 (Turnhout 1967)
R: *ALW* 10.2 (1968) 552-3: A. Kurzeja.

F.19.10
John Beleth: Douteil, Heribert, ed. *Summa de ecclesiasticis officiis.* 2 vols. Corpus Christianorum, continuatio medievalis 41, 41A (Turnhout 1976)
[in PL 202.9-166 titled *Rationale divinorum officiorum*]
R: *Bulletin de littérature ecclésiastique* 80 (1979) 63-4: A.-G. Martimort.

F.19.11
Praepositinus of Cremona: Corbett, James A., ed. *Praepositini Cremonensis tractatus de officiis* (Notre Dame 1969)
R: *JTS* n.s. 21 (1970) 499-501: J.H. Crehan.
F.19.12
William of Melitona: Van Dijk, S.J.P. 'De fontibus *Opusculi super missam* Fr. Guil. de Melitona, O.F.M.,' *EL* 53 (1939) 291-349.
F.19.13
Durandus of Mende: *Rationale divinum officiorum*
There is no modern edition, only a French translation by Charles Barthélemy in 5 volumes (Paris 1854) and an English translation of Book I by J.M. Neale and B. Webb, *The Symbolism of Churches and Church Ornaments* (London 1843), and of Book III by Thomas H. Passmore, *The Sacred Vestments* (London 1899).
F.19.14
Jean de Vignay: Frere, Walter H., ed. 'Exposition de la messe' *from* La Légende dorée *of Jean de Vignay*. ACC 2 (London 1899).

Liturgical Drama

F.20.1
Chambers, Edmund K. *The Medieval Stage*. 2 vols. (Oxford 1903; repr. 1963).
F.20.2
Young, Karl. *The Drama of the Medieval Church*. 2 vols. (Oxford 1933; repr. 1951).
F.20.3
Donovan, Richard B. *The Liturgical Drama in Medieval Spain*. Studies and Texts 4 (Toronto 1958).
F.20.4
Hardison, Osborne B. *Christian Rite and Christian Drama in the Middle Ages* (Baltimore 1965)
R: *Medium Ævum* 36 (1967) 289-92: J. Stevens.
F.20.5
De Boor, Helmut. *Die Textgeschichte der lateinischen Osterfeiern*, Hermaea 22 (Tübingen 1967)
R: *Speculum* 44 (1969) 452-5: O.B. Hardison, Jr.

F.20.6

Stemmler, Theo. *Liturgische Feiern und geistliche Spiele: Studien zu Erscheinungsformen des Dramatischen im Mittelalter.* Buchreihe der Anglia 15 (Tübingen 1970)
R: *Speculum* 47 (1972) 356-61: E. Simon.

F.20.7

Dolan, Diane. *Le Drame liturgique de Pâques en Normandie et en Angleterre au moyen âge.* Publications de l'Université de Poitiers, Lettres et sciences humaines 16 (Paris 1975)
R: *Speculum* 52 (1977) 652-4: O.B. Hardison, Jr.

F.20.8

Berger, Blandine-D. *Le Drame liturgique de Pâques du Xe au XIIIe siècle.* Théologie historique 37 (Paris 1976)
R: *RB* 86 (1976) 353: P.-M. Bogaert.

Early Western
(Non-Roman) Liturgy

(North) African

G.1.1
Rötzer, Wunibald. *Des heiligen Augustinus Schriften als liturgiegeschichtliche Quelle* (Munich 1930).
G.1.2
Gamber, K. 'Das Eucharistiegebet in der frühen nordafrikanischen Liturgie' in *Liturgica* III. Scripta et documenta 17 (Montserrat 1966) 51-65.
G.1.3
Saxer, Victor. *Vie liturgique et quotidienne à Carthage vers le milieu du iiie siècle: Le Témoignage de S. Cyprien et des ses contemporains d'Afrique.*
Studi di antichità cristiana 29 (Rome 1969)
R: *AB* 91 (1973) 462-3: B. de Gaiffier.
G.1.4
Schweitzer, E. 'Fragen der Liturgie in Nordafrika zur Zeit Cyprians,' *ALW* 12 (1970) 69-84.
G.1.5
Coppo, A. 'Vita cristiana e terminologia liturgica a Cartagine verso la metà del iii secolo,' *EL* 85 (1971) 70-86.

Milanese

PATRISTIC ORIGINS

G.2.1
Ambrose (St.) *De sacramentis.* Available in several eds., esp. those of O.
Faller, Corpus scriptorum ecclesiasticorum Latinorum 73 (Vienna 1955),
and B. Botte, Sources chrétiennes 25 bis, 2nd ed. (Paris 1961); and transla-
tions, esp. that of T. Thompson, Translations of Christian Literature, ser.
iii (London 1919; rev. ed. 1950, with translation of *De mysteriis*).
G.2.2
Paredi, A. 'La Liturgia di S. Ambrogio' in *Sant'Ambrogio nel XVI centenario*
(Milan 1940) 71-157.
G.2.3
Beumer, J. 'Die ältesten Zeugnisse für die römische Eucharistiefeier bei
Ambrosius,' *ZKT* 95 (1973) 311-24.

'AMBROSIAN'

Cf. *DACL* **A.2.2**, 1.1373-1442; King, *Primatial* **A.2.11**, 286-456;
Lewandowski **E.10.3**, W. Bishop **G.6.20**.

G.3.1
Heiming, Odilo, ed. *Das* Sacramentarium triplex: *Die Hs. C43 der Zentral-
bibliothek Zürich (Corpus Ambrosiano-Liturgicum I).* LQF 49 (Münster
1968)
R: *JTS* n.s. 20 (1969) 654-7: G.G. Willis.
G.3.2
Heiming, Odilo, ed. *Das Ambrosianische Sakramentar von Biasca (Corpus
Ambrosiano-Liturgicum II).* LQF 51 (Münster 1969)
R: *Theologische Literaturzeitung* 95 (1970) 303-5: W. Nagel.
G.3.3
Frei, Judith, ed. *Das Ambrosianische Sakramentar D3-3 aus dem Mailänd-
ischen Metropolitankapitel (Corpus Ambrosiano-Liturgicum III).* LQF 56
(Münster 1974)
R: *Theologische Literaturzeitung* 100 (1975) 792-4: W. Nagel.

G.3.4
Paredi, Angelo, ed. 'Sacramentarium Ariberti' in *Miscellanea Adriano Bernareggi*. Monumenta Bergomensia 1 (Bergamo 1958) 329-488
R: *Revue des sciences religieuses* 33 (1959) 285-7: R. Amiet.

G.3.5
Paredi, Angelo, ed. *Sacramentarium Bergomense*. Monumenta Bergomensia 6 (Bergamo 1962)
R: *SE* 13 (1962) 62-6: F. Combaluzier (review article).

G.3.6
Indices for the two works above by Fernand Combaluzier, *Sacramentaires de Bergame et d'Ariberto: Table des matières, index des formules*. Instrumenta patristica 5 (Steenbrugge 1962)
On this see F. Dell' Oro, *EL* 77 (1963) 109-14.

G.3.7
Mercati, Giovanni, ed. *Antiche reliquie liturgiche Ambrosiane e Romane*. ST 7 (Rome 1902).

G.3.8
Cagin, Paul, ed. *Antiphonarium Ambrosianum du Musée britannique (xiie siècle)*. Paléographie musicale 5-6 (Paris 1896-1900).

G.3.9
Magistretti, Marco, ed. *Pontificale in usum ecclesiae Mediolanensis necnon ordines Ambrosiani ex codicibus saec. ix-xv*. Monumenta veteris liturgiae Ambrosianae 1 (Milan 1897).

G.3.10
Magistretti, Marco, ed. *Beroldus, sive ecclesiae Ambrosianae Mediolanensis kalendarium et ordines saec. xii*. Manuale Ambrosianum 1 (Milan 1904; repr. Farnborough 1968).

G.3.11
Magistretti, Marco, ed. *Manuale Ambrosianum ex codice saec. xi olim in usum canonicae Vallis Travaliae*. 2 vols. Monumenta veteris liturgiae Ambrosianae 2-3 (Milan 1904).

G.3.12
Borella, Pietro. *Il rito ambrosiano* (Brescia 1964)
R: *ALW* 9.1 (1965) 330-31: O. Heiming.

G.3.13
Wilmart, A. 'Une Exposition de la messe ambrosienne,' *JLW* 2 (1922) 47-67.

G.3.14
Heiming, O. 'Ein "fusionniertes" Gregorianum und ein Ambrosiano-Benedictinum,' *EL* 64 (1950) 238-73.
G.3.15
Heiming, O. 'Die ältesten ungedruckten Kalender der mailändischen Kirche' in *Colligere fragmenta* (see A.4.8) 214-35.
G.3.16
Huglo, Michel et al. *Fonti e paleografia del canto ambrosiano.* Archivio ambrosiano 7 (Milan 1956).
G.3.17
Amiet, R. 'La Tradition manuscrite du missel ambrosien,' *Scriptorium* 14 (1960) 16-60.
G.3.18
Heiming, O. 'Ein benediktinisch-ambrosianisches Gebetbuch des frühen 11. Jahrhunderts,' *ALW* 8.2 (1964) 325-435.
G.3.19
Heiming, O. 'Kleinere Beiträge zur Geschichte der ambrosianischen Liturgie,' *ALW* 12 (1970) 130-47, 13 (1971) 133-40.

Other North Italian

Cf. King, *Past* A.2.12, 1-51; Vanhengel E.2.3.

G.4.1
Lambot, Cyrille, ed. *North Italian Services of the Eleventh Century.* HBS 67 (London 1931)
These are *ordines.*
G.4.2
Benz, Suitbert. *Der Rotulus von Ravenna nach seiner Herkunft und seiner Bedeutung für die Liturgiegeschichte kritisch untersucht.* LQF 45 (Münster 1967)
R: *RHE* 63 (1968) 89-91: B. Botte. Cf. A. Olivar, 'Abermals der *Rotulus* von Ravenna,' *ALW* 11 (1969) 40-58; and Benz, 'Nochmals der *Rotulus* von Ravenna: Eine Gegenkritik,' *ALW* 13 (1971) 213-20.
G.4.3
Cabrol, F. 'Autour de la liturgie de Ravenne: Saint Pierre Chrysologue et le *Rotulus*,' *RB* 23 (1906) 489-500.

G.4.4
Gamber, K. 'Der *Ordo Romanus IV*, ein Dokument der ravennatischen Liturgie des 8. Jahrhunderts,' *Römische Quartalschrift* 66 (1971) 154-70.
G.4.5
Rehle, S. 'Ein Plenarmissale des 9. Jahrhunderts aus Oberitalien,' *SE* 21 (1972-73) 291-321.

Beneventan and South Italian

Cf. King, *Past* A.2.12, 52-76.

G.5.1
Rehle, Sieghild, ed. Missale Beneventanum *von Canosa.* Textus patristici et liturgici 9 (Regensburg 1972)
R: *AB* 92 (1974) 248-9: B. de Gaiffier.
G.5.2
Rehle, S. '*Missale Beneventanum* (Codex VI.33 des erzbischöflichen Archivs von Benevent),' *SE* 21 (1972-73) 323-405.
G.5.3
Dold, Alban, ed. *Die Zürcher und Peterlinger Messbuch-Fragmente aus der Zeit der Jahrtausendwende im Bari-Schrifttyp.* TA 25 (Beuron 1934).
G.5.4
Dold, A. 'Umfangreiche Reste zweien Plenarmissalien des 11. und 12. Jhts. aus Monte Cassino,' *EL* 53 (1939) 111-67.
G.5.5
Hesbert, Réné-Jean, ed. *Graduel bénéventain: Le Codex 10673 de la Bibliothèque Vaticane, fonds latin. xie siècle.* Paléographie musicale 1st ser. 14 (Tournai 1931-6; repr. Berne 1971).
G.5.6
Hesbert, R.-J. 'L'*Antiphonale missarum* de l'ancien rit bénéventain,' *EL* 52 (1938) 28-66, 141-58; 53 (1939) 168-90; 59 (1945) 69-95; 60 (1946) 103-141; 61 (1947) 153-210.

Mozarabic (alias Visigothic)

Cf. *DACL* A.2.2, 12.390-491; King, *Primatial* A.2.11, 457-631; Szövérffy
D.7.15, Lewandowski E.10.3, Pinell F.8.9, Bernal F.8.12.

G.6.1
Férotin, Mario, ed. *Le* Liber ordinum *en usage dans l'église wisigothique et
mozarabe de l'Espagne du cinquième au onzième siècle.* Monumenta
ecclesiae liturgica 5 (Paris 1904).
G.6.2
Férotin, Mario, ed. *Le* Liber Mozarabicus sacramentorum *et les manuscrits
mozarabes.* Monumenta ecclesiae liturgica 6 (Paris 1912).
G.6.3
Perez de Urbel, Justo and A. Gonzalez y Ruiz-Zorrilla, eds. *Liber commicus
sive lectionarius missae.* MHS 2-3 (Madrid 1950-55)
This supplants the edition by Germain Morin (Maredsous 1893).
G.6.4
Mundó, Anscari M. 'El Commicus palimsest Paris lat. 2269: Amb notes
sobre litúrgia i manuscrits visigótics a Septimània i Catalunya' in *Liturgica,*
I. Scripta et documenta 7 (Montserrat 1956) 151-275.
G.6.5
Fernandez de la Cuesta, Ismael, ed. *El* Breviarium Gothicum *de Silos
(Archivo monastico MS. 6).* MHS 8 (Madrid-Barcelona 1965); = *HS* 17
(1964) 393-494
R: *EL* 81 (1967) 167: V. Raffa.
G.6.6
Vives, Jose, ed. *Oracional visigótico.* MHS 1 (Barcelona 1946).
G.6.7
Gilson, Julius P., ed. *The Mozarabic Psalter (British Museum MS. Add.
30851).* HBS 30 (London 1905).
G.6.8
Fábrega Grau, Ángel, ed. *Pasionario hispánico (siglos vii-xi).* 2 vols. MHS 6
(Madrid 1953-5).
G.6.9
Brou, Louis and Jose Vives, eds. *Antifonario visigotico mozarabe de la
catedral de Leon.* MHS 5/1 and [facsimiles] 5/2 (Barcelona-Madrid-León
1959 and 1953)
This supplants the edition by the Benedictines of Silos (León 1928).

G.6.10
Blume, Clemens, ed. *Hymnodia Gotica: Die mozarabischen Hymnen des alt-spanischen Ritus.* Analecta hymnica medii aevi 27 (Leipzig 1897).
G.6.11
Pinell, Jorge M., ed. *Liber orationum psalmographus: Colectas de salmos del antiguo rito hispanico.* MHS 9 (Barcelona and Madrid 1972)
R: *EL* 87 (1973) 284-300: A.M. Triacca; *JTS* n.s. 24 (1973) 601-2: H. Ashworth.
G.6.12
Ortiz, Alfonso, ed. *Missale mixtum secundum regulam beati Isidori* (Toledo 1500; newly ed. by A. Lesley, Rome 1755; this ed. repr. in PL 85).
G.6.13
Ortiz, A., ed. *Breviarium secundum regulam beati Isidori* (Toledo 1502; newly ed. by Card. F. A. de Lorenzana, Madrid 1775; this ed. repr. in PL 86).
G.6.14
On the above two celebrated editions, in which so much later medieval material was passed off as 'Mozarabic,' see L. Brou, 'Etudes sur le missel et le bréviaire "mozarabes" imprimés,' *HS* 11 (1958) 349-98.
G.6.15
Rivera Recio, Juan F., ed. *Estudios sobre la liturgia mozarabe* (Toledo 1965)
The most useful compendium of information currently available, including a list of sources by J.M. Pinell (pages 109-64) and a general bibliography by J.M. Mora Ontalva (pages 165-87).
G.6.16
Brou, L. 'Bulletin de liturgie mozarabe 1936-48,' *HS* 2 (1949) 459-84.
G.6.17
Pinell, J.M. 'Boletín de liturgia hispano-visigótica (1949-1956),' *HS* 9 (1956) 405-28.
G.6.18
Mora Ontalva, J.M. de, 'Nuevo boletín de liturgia hispánica antigua,' *HS* 26 (1973) 209-37.
G.6.19
Whitehill, W.M. 'A Catalogue of Mozarabic Liturgical Manuscripts containing the Psalter and *Liber canticorum*,' *JLW* 14 (1934) 95-122.

G.6.20
Bishop, William C. *The Mozarabic and Ambrosian Rites.* Alcuin Club Tracts 15 (London 1924) 1-97.
G.6.21
Prado, Germán. *Historia del rito mozárabe y Toledano* (Silos 1928).
G.6.22
Porter, W.S. 'Studies in the Mozarabic Office,' *JTS* 35 (1934) 266-86.
G.6.23
Baumstark, A. 'Orientalisches in altspanischer Liturgie,' *Oriens Christianus* 3rd ser. 10 (1935) 3-37.
G.6.24
David, Pierre. *Etudes historiques sur la Galice et le Portugal du vi^e au xiie siècle* (Paris-Lisbon 1947)
Review article by L. Brou, 'Liturgie "mozarabe" ou liturgie "hispanique",' *EL* 63 (1949) 66-70.
G.6.25
Krinke, J. 'Der spanische Taufritus im frühen Mittelalter,' *Gesammelte Aufsätze zur Kulturgeschichte Spaniens* 9 (1954) 33-116.
G.6.26
Pinell, J.M. 'Vestigis del lucernari a Occident' in *Liturgica*, I. Scripta et documenta 7 (Montserrat 1956) 91-149
Cf. J. Bernal, 'Primeros vestigos de lucernario en España' in *Liturgica*, III. Scripta et documenta 17 (Montserrat 1966) 21-49.
G.6.27
Pinell, J.M. 'El oficio hispano-visigotico,' *HS* 10 (1957) 385-427.
G.6.28
Pinell, J.M. 'Fragmentos de códices del antiguo rito hispánico,' *HS* 17 (1964) 195-229, 25 (1972) 185-208.
G.6.29
Rovalo, P. 'Temporal y santoral en el Adviento visigodo. Su relación a través del oficio,' *HS* 19 (1966) 243-320.
G.6.30
Pinell, J.M. 'Las horas vigilares del oficio monacal hispánico' in *Liturgica*, III. Scripta et documenta 17 (Montserrat 1966) 197-340.
G.6.31
Akeley, Thomas C. *Christian Initiation in Spain c. 300-1100* (London 1967)
R: *AB* 87 (1969) 473-4: B. de Gaiffier, with reservations.

G.6.32
Randel, Don M. *The Responsorial Psalm Tones for the Mozarabic Office.*
Princeton Studies in Music 3 (Princeton 1969)
R: *Musical Quarterly* 55 (1969) 575-80: R. Steiner.
G.6.33
Janini, J. 'Officia Silensia,' *HS* 29 (1976) 325-81, 30 (1977) 331-418.

Celtic
(especially Irish to c. 1172)

Cf. *DACL* A.2.2, 2.2969-3032; King, *Past* A.2.12, 186-275.

G.7.1
Warner, George F., ed. *The Stowe Missal.* 2 vols. HBS 31-2 (London 1906-
1915).
G.7.2
MacCarthy, Bartholomew. 'On the Stowe Missal,' *Royal Irish Academy
Transactions* 27 (1886) 135-268.
G.7.3
Dold, Alban and Leo Eizenhöfer, eds. *Das irische Palimpsestsakramentar im
Clm. 14429.* TA 53-4 (Beuron 1964)
R: *Theologisches Revue* 62 (1966) 49-51: K. Gamber; *EL* 79 (1965) 144-5:
H. Ashworth
Cf. Eizenhöfer's supplementary notes in *SE* 17 (1966) 355-64.
G.7.4
Warren, Frederick E., ed. *The Antiphonary of Bangor.* 2 vols. HBS 4, 10
(London 1893, 1895).
G.7.5
Bernard, John H. and Robert Atkinson, eds. *The Irish* Liber hymnorum.
HBS 13-14 (London 1898).
G.7.6
Stokes, Whitley, ed. *The Martyrology of Oengus the Culdee.* HBS 29
(London 1905).
G.7.7
Lawlor, Hugh J., ed. *The Psalter and Martyrology of Ricemarch.* 2 vols.
HBS 47-8 (London 1914).

G.7.8
Warren, Frederick E. *The Liturgy and Ritual of the Celtic Church* (Oxford 1881)
Still astonishingly useful, despite its age; includes many fragments of texts.
G.7.9
Bishop, E. 'Spanish Symptoms' in *Liturgica historica* (see **A.4.1**) 165-202.
First publ. 1907.
G.7.10
Hennig, J. 'Studies in the Liturgy of the Early Irish Church,' *Irish Ecclesiastical Record* 75 (1951) 318-33.
G.7.11
Ryan, John. 'The Mass in the Early Irish Church,' *Studies, an Irish Quarterly Review* 50 (1961) 371-84.

Gallican

Cf. *DACL* **A.2.2**, 6.i.473-593; King, *Past* **A.2.12**, 77-185; Duchesne **B.1.2**, ET 189-227; Vanhengel **E.2.3**.

G.8.1
Mabillon, Jean. *De liturgia Gallicana* (Paris 1685; repr. PL 72.99-448).
G.8.2
Gerbert, Martin. *Monumenta veteris liturgiae Alemannicae* (St. Blasien 1777).
G.8.3
Neale, John Mason and G.H. Forbes, eds. *The Ancient Liturgies of the Gallican Church* (Burntisland 1855-7; repr. New York 1970)
Reprints earlier editions of the 'Masses of Mone,' *Missale Gothicum, Missale Gallicanum vetus,* and *Bobbio Missal* (on all of which, see below).
G.8.4
Ratcliff, Edward C., ed. *Expositio antiquae liturgiae Gallicanae.* HBS 98 (London 1971)
R: *ALW* 16 (1974) 421-2: A. Kurzeja.
G.8.5
Batiffol, Pierre. 'L'*Expositio liturgiae Gallicanae* attribuée à S. Germain de Paris' in *Etudes de liturgie et d'archéologie chrétiennes* (Paris 1919) 245-90.

G.8.6
Van der Mensbrugghe, A. 'Pseudo-Germanus Reconsidered' in *Studia patristica*, V. Texte und Untersuchungen 80 (Berlin 1962) 172-84.
G.8.7
Dold, Alban, ed. *Das älteste Liturgiebuch der lateinischen Kirche: Ein altgallikanisches Lektionar des 5/6. Jahrhundert.* TA 26-8 (Beuron 1936).
G.8.8
Gamber, Klaus, ed. *Ordo antiquus Gallicanus: Der gallikanische Messritus des 6. Jahrhunderts.* Textus patristici et liturgici 3 (Regensburg 1965).
G.8.9
Dold, Alban, ed. *Das Sakramentar im Schabcodex M 12 sup. der Bibliotheca Ambrosiana.* TA 43 (Beuron 1952).
G.8.10
Bannister, Henry M., ed. *Missale Gothicum: A Gallican Sacramentary.* HBS 52, 54 (London 1917, 1919).
G.8.11
Mohlberg, Leo Cunibert, ed. *Missale Gothicum.* RED, series maior 5 (Rome 1961)
R: *EL* 76 (1962) 74-81: F. Dell' Oro. For a concordance, see **H.1.6.**
G.8.12
Lowe, Elias A. et al., eds. *The Bobbio Missal.* HBS 53 [facsimile], 58 [text], 61 [notes and studies by A. Wilmart, H.A. Wilson, and Lowe] (London 1917, 1920, 1924).
G.8.13
Mohlberg, Leo Cunibert et al., eds. *Missale Francorum.* RED, series maior 2 (Rome 1957).
G.8.14
Mohlberg, Leo Cunibert et al., eds. *Missale Gallicanum vetus.* RED, series maior 3 (Rome 1958)
This edition includes several fragmentary texts and the oldest of Gallican mass formularies, the 'Masses of Mone' (first published by F.J. Mone in 1850). Cf. Wilmart **G.8.15.**
G.8.15
Wilmart, A. 'L'Age et l'ordre des messes de Mone,' *RB* 28 (1911) 377-90.
G.8.16
Duchesne, L. 'Sur l'origine de la liturgie gallicane,' *Revue d'histoire et de littérature religieuse* 5 (1900) 31-47.

G.8.17
Thibaut, J.-B. *L'Ancienne Liturgie gallicane: Son origine et sa formation en Provence aux ve et vi^e siècles sous l'influence de Cassien et de Saint Césaire d'Arles* (Paris 1929).
G.8.18
Quasten, J. 'Oriental Influence in the Gallican Liturgy,' *Traditio* 1 (1943) 55-78.
G.8.19
Griffe, E. 'Aux origines de la liturgie gallicane,' *Bulletin de littérature ecclésiastique* 52 (1951) 17-43.
G.8.20
Ashworth, H. 'Gregorian Elements in Some Early Gallican Service Books,' *Traditio* 13 (1957) 431-43.
G.8.21
Porter, William S. *The Gallican Rite*. Studies in Eucharistic Faith and Practice 4 (London 1958).

Early Monastic

Cf. Heiming **D.3.2**, Loew **F.2.4**.

G.9.1
Nussbaum, Otto. *Kloster, Priestermönch, und Privatmesse: Ihr Verhältnis im Westen, von den Anfängen bis zum hohen Mittelalter*. Theophaneia 14 (Bonn 1961)
R: *ZKT* 85 (1963) 75-83: A. Häussling.
G.9.2
Häussling, Angelus A. *Mönchskonvent und Eucharistiefeier: Eine Studie über die Messe in der abendländischen Klosterliturgie des frühen Mittelalters und zur Geschichte der Messhäufigkeit*. LQF 58 (Münster 1973)
R: *JTS* n.s. 26 (1975) 199-200: R.J. Halliburton.
G.9.3
Lowe, E.A. 'An Unknown Latin Psalter on Mount Sinai,' *Scriptorium* 9 (1955) 177-99; and 'Two Other Unknown Latin Liturgical Fragments on Mount Sinai,' *Scriptorium* 19 (1965) 3-29. Cf. Gribomont **G.9.4**.
G.9.4
Gribomont, J. 'Le Mystérieux Calendrier latin du Sinai: Edition et commentaire,' *AB* 75 (1957) 105-34.

Early Roman Liturgy
and Derivatives

'Roman' Sacramentaries

GENERAL

It seems most helpful here to give, after a few general works, the principal editions of, and literature concerning, the best-known sacramentaries under the customary Leonine-Gelasian-Gregorian nomenclature, unsatisfactory as that is. In the interests of clarity and easy access to reference works, the shelf-mark of the manuscript most closely involved will be indicated wherever possible. Fundamental as sources of further reference are the comprehensive surveys of Dekkers A.6.1, Vogel A.6.3, Gamber A.6.2, and Leroquais C.2.3.

H.1.1
Delisle, Léopold. *Mémoire sur d'anciens sacramentaires.* Mémoires Academie des inscriptions et belles-lettres 32 pt. 1 (Paris 1886); = pp. 57-423.
H.1.2
Probst, Ferdinand. *Die ältesten römischen Sakramentarien und* Ordines (Münster 1892).
H.1.3
Bourque, Emmanuel. *Etude sur les sacramentaires romains,* pt. i: *Les Textes primitifs* (Rome 1948); pt. ii: *Les Textes remaniés.* 2 vols. (Quebec 1952; Rome 1958).
H.1.4
Gamber, Klaus et al. *Sakramentartypen: Versuch einer Gruppierung der Handschriften und Fragmente bis zur Jahrtausendwende.* TA 49-50 (Beuron 1958)

This important work has been attacked on grounds of over-rigid and over-ambitious classification; see, for example, the review by B. Botte in *RHE* 55 (1960) 516-17.

H.1.5
Wilson, Henry A. *A Classified Index to the Leonine, Gelasian, and Gregorian Sacramentaries* (Cambridge 1892).

H.1.6
Siffrin, Petrus. *Konkordanztabellen zu den römischen Sakramentarien*, I: *Sacramentarium Veronense;* II: *Liber sacramentorum Romanae aeclesiae* [Gelasianum] ; III: *Missale Gothicum*. RED, series minor: Subsidia studiorum 4-6 (Rome 1958-61).

'LEONINE' (*ALIAS* 'VERONESE')

Cf. Saxer **F.13.7.**

H.2.1
Feltoe, Charles L., ed. *Sacramentarium Leonianum* (Cambridge 1896).

H.2.2
Mohlberg, Leo Cunibert et al., eds. *Sacramentarium Veronense*. RED, series maior 1 (Rome 1956)
This more accurate title derives from the sole MS, Verona, Cod. Bibl. Cap. LXXXV (80).

H.2.3
Capelle, B. 'Messes du pape S. Gélase dans le sacramentaire léonien,' *RB* 56 (1945-6) 12-41; and 'Retouches gélasiennes dans le sacramentaire léonien,' *RB* 61 (1951) 3-14.

H.2.4
Callewaert, C. 'Saint Léon le Grand et les textes du Léonien,' *SE* 1 (1948) 35-122.

H.2.5
Stuiber, Alfred. *Libelli sacramentorum Romani: Untersuchung zur Entstehung des sogennanten* Sacramentarium Leonianum. Theophaneia 6 (Bonn 1950).

H.2.6
Chavasse, A. 'Messes du pape Vigile (537-555) dans le sacramentaire léonien,' *EL* 64 (1950) 161-213, 66 (1952) 145-215.

H.2.7

Coebergh, C. 'S. Gélase Ier auteur principal du soi-disant sacramentaire léonien,' *EL* 64 (1950) 214-37; ' ... de plusieurs messes et prières du sacr. léon.,' *EL* 65 (1951) 171-81; ' ... de plusieurs messes et préfaces du soi-disant sacr. léon.,' *SE* 4 (1952) 46-102.

H.2.8

Hope, David M. *The Leonine Sacramentary: A Reassessment of its Nature and Purpose* (Oxford 1971)
R: *JTS* n.s. 23 (1972) 510-12: H. Ashworth [reservations]; *JEH* 23 (1972) 370-71: R.C.D. Jasper.

'OLDER' GELASIAN

H.3.1

Wilson, Henry A., ed. *The Gelasian Sacramentary* (Oxford 1894).

H.3.2

Mohlberg, Leo Cunibert, ed. *Liber sacramentorum Romanae aeclesiae ordini anni circuli.* RED, series maior 4 (Rome 1960). Vat. Reg. 316.
R: *EL* 74 (1960) 461-3: J. Deshusses.

H.3.3

Dold, Alban and Leo Eizenhöfer, eds. *Das Prager Sakramentar (Cod. O.83).* TA 38-42 (Beuron 1949)
This sacramentary fits here only very roughly.

H.3.4

Bishop, E. 'The Earliest Roman Mass Book (the *Gelasianum*)' in *Liturgica historica* (see **A.4.1**) 39-61. First publ. 1894, as a review of Wilson's ed.

H.3.5

Lang, Arthur P. *Leo der Grosse und die Texte des Altgelasianums: Mit Berücksichtigung des* Sacramentarium Leonianum *und des* Sacramentarium Gregorianum (Steyl 1957)
R: *JTS* n.s. 9 (1958) 382-6: J.H. Crehan.

H.3.6

Chavasse, Antoine. *Le Sacramentaire gélasien (Vaticanus Reginensis 316): Sacramentaire presbytéral en usage dans les titres romains au viie siècle* (Paris-Tournai 1958).

H.3.7

On the above, see B. Capelle, 'Origine et vicissitudes du sacr. gélas. d'après un livre récent,' *RHE* 54 (1959) 864-79.

H.3.8
Gamber, K. 'Das kampanische Messbuch als Vorläufer des Gelasianum. Ist der hl. Paulinus von Nola der Verfasser?' *SE* 12 (1961) 5-111.

EIGHTH-CENTURY GELASIAN
('JUNGGELASIANA')

H.4.1
Moreton, Bernard. *The Eighth-Century Gelasian Sacramentary* (Oxford 1976)
R: *ALW* 19 (1977) 694: B. Neunheuser.
H.4.2
Mohlberg, Leo Cunibert, ed. *Das fränkische* Sacramentarium Gelasianum *in alamannischer Überlieferung.* LQF 1-2 (Münster 1918; 2nd ed. 1939). St. Gall 348.
H.4.3
Cagin, Paul, ed. with Léopold Delisle. *Sacramentaire gélasien d'Angoulême* (Angoulême 1918). Paris, B.N. lat. 816
'Index analytique' by F. Combaluzier, *EL* 66 (1952) 1*-15*.
H.4.4
Mohlberg, Leo Cunibert, ed. 'Un sacramentario palinsesto del secolo viii dell' Italia centrale,' *Rendiconti della Pontificia Accademia Romana di archeologia* 3 (1925) 391-450.
H.4.5
De Puniet, Pierre, ed. *Le Sacramentaire romain de Gellone.* Bibliotheca 'Ephemerides liturgicae' 4 (Rome 1938; also publ. separately in *EL*, 1934-8) Outlines and tables, not a full edition of the manuscript, Paris, B.N. lat. 12048.
H.4.6
Hänggi, Anton and A. Schönherr, eds. *Sacramentarium Rhenaugiense: Handschrift Rh 30 der Zentralbibliothek Zürich.* SF 15 (Fribourg 1970) Important review by M.B. Moreton in *JTS* n.s. 22 (1971) 626-31.
H.4.7
Rehle, Sieghild, ed. Sacramentarium Gelasianum mixtum *von Saint-Amand.* Textus patristici et liturgici 10 (Regensburg 1973). Paris, B.N. lat. 2296, formerly Colbert 1348
R: *RB* 84 (1974) 419-20: P. Verbraken.

H.4.8
De Puniet, P. 'Le Sacramentaire gélasien de la Collection Phillipps (fin du viiie s.): I, Son propre nationale; II, Son propre nationale et ses emprunts au léonien,' *EL* 43 (1929) 91-109, 280-303.

H.4.9
Bourque, Emmanuel. *Etudes sur les sacramentaires romains,* pt. ii, vol. I: *Le Gélasien du viiie siècle* (Quebec 1952).

H.4.10
Chavasse, A. 'Le Sacramentaire gélasien du viiie siècle: Ses deux principales formes,' *EL* 73 (1959) 249-98.

H.4.11
Deshusses, J. 'Le Sacramentaire de Gellone dans son contexte historique,' *EL* 75 (1961) 193-210.

H.4.12
Gamber, K. 'Heimat und Ausbildung der Gelasiana saec. viii (Junggelasiana),' *SE* 14 (1963) 99-129.

GREGORIAN

H.5.1
Wilson, Henry A., ed. *The Gregorian Sacramentary under Charles the Great.* HBS 49 (London 1915).

H.5.2
Lietzmann, Hans. *Das* Sacramentarium Gregorianum *nach der Aachener Urexemplar.* LQF 3 (Münster 1921; repr. 1967).

H.5.3
Mohlberg, Leo Cunibert, ed. *Die älteste erreichbare Gestalt des* Liber sacramentorum anni circuli *der römischen Kirche (Cod. Padua D. 47),* with an essay by A. Baumstark. LQF 11-12 (Münster 1927; repr. 1967 with supplement by O. Heiming).

H.5.4
Deshusses, Jean, ed. *Le Sacramentaire grégorien, ses principales formes d'après les plus anciens manuscrits,* I: *Le Sacramentaire, le supplément d'Aniane.* SF 16 (Fribourg 1971); II: *Textes complémentaires pour la messe.* SF 24 (Fribourg 1979)
R: *JTS* n.s. 23 (1972) 261-4: M.B. Moreton.

H.5.5

Dold, Alban, ed. *Ein vorhadrianisches gregorianisches Palimpsest-Sakramentar in Gold-Unzialschrift.* TA 5 (Beuron 1919).

H.5.6

Gamber, Klaus, with A. Dold. *Wege zum Urgregorianum: Erörterung der Grundfragen und Rekonstruktionsversuch des Sakramentars Gregors des Grossen vom Jahre 592.* TA 46 (Beuron 1956).

H.5.7

Gamber, Klaus. *Sacramentarium Gregorianum,* pt. i: *Das Stationsmessbuch des Papstes Gregor;* pt. ii: *Appendix, Sontags- und Votivmessen.* Textus patristici et liturgici 4, 6 (Regensburg 1966, 1967)
R: *EL* 81 (1967) 161-3: V. Raffa, and 82 (1968) 55-8: A.M. Triacca.

H.5.8

Dold, Alban and Klaus Gamber, eds. *Das Sakramentar von Salzburg: Seinem Typus nach auf Grund der erhaltenen Fragmente rekonstruiert in seinem Verhältnis zum Paduanum untersucht.* TA Beiheft 4 (Beuron 1960)
R: *EL* 75 (1961) 376-8: V. Raffa.

H.5.9

Bourque, Emmanuel. *Etude sur les sacramentaires romains,* pt. ii, vol. II: *Le Sacramentaire d'Hadrien: Le Supplément d'Alcuin et les grégoriens mixtes.* Studi di antichità cristiana 25 (Rome 1958)
On this, see P. Borella, 'Dal sacramentario gregoriano al messale romano,' *EL* 75 (1961) 237-43. Also relevant are pages 299-391 of volume I of Bourque's work: *Les Textes primitifs,* Studi di antichità cristiana 20 (Rome 1948).

H.5.10

Wilmart, A. 'Un Missel grégorien ancien,' *RB* 26 (1909) 281-300.

H.5.11

Brou, L. 'Le Sacramentaire de Nonantola,' *EL* 64 (1950) 274-82.

H.5.12

Amiet, R. 'Le Prologue *Hucusque* et la table des *Capitula* du supplément d'Alcuin au sacramentaire grégorien,' *Scriptorium* 7 (1953) 177-209.

H.5.13

Amiet, R. 'Le Plus Ancien Témoin du supplément d'Alcuin,' *EL* 72 (1958) 97-110.

H.5.14

Deshusses, J. 'Le "Supplément" au sacramentaire grégorien: Alcuin ou S. Benoît d'Aniane?' *ALW* 9.1 (1965) 48-71.

H.5.15
Barré, H. and J. Deshusses. 'A la recherche du missel d'Alcuin,' *EL* 82 (1968) 3-44.

H.5.16
Deshusses, J. 'Les Messes d'Alcuin,' *ALW* 14 (1972) 7-41.

H.5.17
Ashworth, H. 'The Influence of the Lombard Invasions on the Gregorian Sacramentary,' *Bulletin of the John Rylands Library* 36 (1953-4) 305-27.

H.5.18
Ashworth, H. 'Did St. Gregory Compose a Sacramentary?' in *Studia patristica*, II. Texte und Untersuchungen 63 (Berlin 1957) 3-16.

H.5.19
Coebergh, C. 'La Messe de S. Grégoire dans le sacramentaire d'Hadrien: Essai d'explication d'une anomalie notoire, suivie de remarques sur la Mémoire des defunts et le développement du culte des Saints Confesseurs à Rome du ve au viiie siècle,' *SE* 12 (1961) 372-404.

H.5.20
Pluta, A. 'Inwieweit kann man von "Entstellung" im *Sacramentarium Gregorianum* des Aachener Archetypus sprechen?' *ALW* 10.1 (1967) 125-41.

H.5.21
Deshusses, J. 'Le Sacramentaire grégorien de Trente,' *RB* 78 (1968) 261-82.

H.5.22
Deshusses, J. 'Le Sacramentaire grégorien pré-hadrianique,' *RB* 80 (1970) 213-37.

H.5.23
Gamber, K. 'Der fränkische Anhang zum Gregorianum im Licht eines Fragments aus dem Anfang des ix. Jhts.,' *SE* 21 (1972-73) 267-89.

H.5.24
Gamber, K. '*Sacramentaria Praehadriana:* Neue Zeugnisse der süddeutschen Überlieferung des vorhadrianischen *Sacramentarium Gregorianum* im 8.-9. Jht.,' *Scriptorium* 27 (1973) 3-15.

GREGORIAN-GELASIAN MIXED

H.6.1
Richter, Gregor and A. Schönfelder, eds. *Sacramentarium Fuldense saeculi X.* Quellen und Abhandlungen zur Geschichte der Abtei und der Diözese Fulda 9 (Fulda 1912). Göttingen, Universitätsbibl. Cod. theol. 231.

H.6.2

Dold, Alban and A. Baumstark, eds. *Das Palimpsestsakramentar im Codex Augiensis cxii: Ein Messbuch ältester Struktur aus dem Alpengebiet.* TA 12 (Beuron 1925).

H.6.3

Brinktrine, Johannes, ed. *Sacramentarium Rossianum.* Römische Quartalschrift Supplementheft 25 (Freiburg 1930). Vat. Ross. lat. 204.

H.6.4

* Pelt, Jean-B., ed. *Le Sacramentaire de Drogon* (Metz 1936). Paris, B.N. lat. 9428.

H.6.5

Gamber, Klaus, ed. *Das Sakramentar von Jena.* TA 52 (Beuron 1962). Jena, Universitätsbibl. Bud. M.f. 366.

NOT CONVINCINGLY CLASSIFIED

H.7.1

Chevalier, Ulysse, ed. 'Sacramentarium abbatiae S. Remigii Remensis' in *Sacramentaire et martyrologe de l'abbaye de Saint-Rémy.* Bibliothèque liturgique 7 (Paris 1900) 305-57.

H.7.2

Dold, Alban and K. Gamber, eds. *Das Sakramentar von Monza im Cod. F.I/101 der dortigen Kapitelsbibliothek.* TA Beiheft 3 (Beuron 1957).

H.7.3

Unterkircher, Franz, ed. *Il sacramentario Adalpretiano: Cod. Vindob. Ser. n.206.* Collana di monografie edita dalla Società per gli studi Trentini 15 (Trent 1966)
R: *EL* 81 (1967) 446-9: A.M. Triacca.

H.7.4

Rehle, Sieghild, ed. *Sacramentarium Arnonis: Die Fragmente des Salzburger Exemplars.* Textus patristici et liturgici 8 (Regensburg 1970). Munich, Clm 29164 I/1a and other fragments
R: *Studi medievali* 3rd ser. 13 (1972) 1126: R. Grégoire.

H.7.5

Gamber, Klaus, ed. *Das Bonifatius-Sakramentar und weitere frühe Liturgiebücher aus Regensburg.* Textus patristici et liturgici 12 (Regensburg 1975)
R: *AB* 94 (1976) 428-9: J. van der Straeten.

Early Medieval Chant Books

Cf. Hesbert **D.6.1.**

H.8.1
Hesbert, Réné-Jean. *Antiphonale missarum sextuplex ... d'après le graduel de Monza et les antiphonaires de Rheinau, du Mont Blandin, de Compiègne, de Corbie, et de Senlis* (Brussels 1935)
A monumental setting-out of the contents of six of the oldest mass-chant codices.

Solesmes, Benedictines of: editions in their series Paléographie musicale (all repr. Berne 1970-) of:
H.8.2
Le Codex 339 de la Bibliothèque de Saint-Gall (xe siècle): Antiphonale missarum S. Gregorii. 1st ser. 1 (Solesmes 1889-90).
H.8.3
Le Codex 121 de la Bibliothèque d'Einsiedeln (x^e-xie siècle): Antiphonale missarum S. Gregorii. 1st ser. 4 (Solesmes 1894-6).
H.8.4
Antiphonale missarum Sancti Gregorii (ixe-xe siècle): Codex 239 de la Bibliothèque de Laon. 1st ser. 10 (Tournai 1909-12).
H.8.5
Antiphonale missarum Sancti Gregorii (xe siècle): Codex 47 de la Bibliothèque de Chartres. 1st ser. 11 (Tournai 1912-15).
H.8.6
Antiphonarium tonale missarum (xie siècle): Codex H.159 de la Bibliothèque de l'Ecole de médecine de Montpellier. 2 vols. 1st ser. 7-8 (Solesmes 1901; Tournai 1901-5).
H.8.7
Antiphonale de Hartker (xe siècle). 2nd ser. 1 (Solesmes 1900; rev. ed. by J. Froger, Berne 1970).
H.8.8
Cantatorium de Saint-Gall (ixe siècle). 2nd ser. 2 (Tournai 1924).

Early Medieval Lectionaries

Cf. Frere H.11.2.

H.9.1

Ranke, Ernst K. *Das kirchliche Perikopensystem* (Berlin 1847)
For a text of the ninth-century *Comes Hieronymi.*

H.9.2

Chapman, John. *Notes on the Early History of the Vulgate Gospels*
(Oxford 1908), ch. vii: 'The Pauline Lectionary of the Codex Fuldensis'
Discusses the oldest extant epistle list, written for Bishop Victor of Capua
c. 545.

H.9.3

Beissel, Stephan. *Entstehung der Perikopen des römischen Messbuches: Zur
Geschichte der Evangelienbücher in der ersten Hälfte des Mittelalters*
(Freiburg 1907; repr. Rome 1967).

H.9.4

Morin, G. 'Le Plus Ancien *Comes* ou lectionnaire de l'église romaine,' *RB*
27 (1910) 41-74; and 'Liturgie et basiliques de Rome au milieu du viie
siècle ...' *RB* 28 (1911) 296-330
On, respectively, the epistolary and evangeliary contained in Würzburg Mp.
th. fol 62.

H.9.5

Wilmart, A. 'Le *Comes* de Murbach,' *RB* 30 (1913) 25-69.

H.9.6

Klauser, Theodor. *Das römische* Capitulare evangeliorum. LQF 28 (Münster
1935).

H.9.7

Wilmart, A. 'Le Lectionnaire d'Alcuin,' *EL* 51 (1937) 136-97. Repr. as
Bibliotheca 'Ephemerides liturgicae' 2 (Rome 1937).

H.9.8

Salmon, Pierre, ed. *Le Lectionnaire de Luxeuil,* I: *Edition et étude comparative;* II: *Etude paléographique et liturgique.* Collectanea biblica Latina 7, 9
(Rome 1944, 1953).

H.9.9

Dold, A. 'Ein Vorläufer des *Comes* von Murbach,' *EL* 65 (1951) 237-52.

Ordines Romani

Cf. Vogel A.6.3, 101-81.

H.10.1
Andrieu, Michel, ed. *Les* Ordines Romani *du haut moyen âge.* 5 vols.
Spicilegium sacrum Lovaniense 11, 23-4, 28-9 (Louvain 1931, 1948-51,
1956-61; repr. 1960-65)
R: of IV-V in *EL* 76 (1962) 69-74: P. Borella
The magisterial edition of the *Ordines,* with full apparatus and indices.
H.10.2
Atchley, Edward G.C.F., ed. and tr. *Ordo Romanus primus.* Library of
Liturgiology and Ecclesiology 6 (London 1905).
H.10.3
Silva-Tarouca, Carlo. 'Giovanni "archicantor" di S. Pietro a Roma e l'*Ordo
Romanus* da lui composto (anno 680),' *Atti della pontificia Accademia
Romana di archeologia, Memorie* 1.ii (1923) 159-219; = *Miscellanea
Giovanni Battista de Rossi* (Rome 1923-4) I, 159-219. St. Gall MS. 349
The attribution to John the Archchanter is generally rejected.
H.10.4
Wilmart, A. 'Notice du "pontifical de Poitiers" (Arsenal 227),' *JLW* 4
(1924) 48-81, with subsequent note in 5 (1925) 159-63
A collection closer in effect to an *Ordo* than to a pontifical.

'Early Roman' Liturgy

H.11.1
Bishop, E. 'The Genius of the Roman Rite' in *Liturgica historica* (see
A.4.1) 1-19.
H.11.2
Frere, Walter H. *Studies in Early Roman Liturgy,* I: *The Kalendar;* II: *The
Roman Gospel-Lectionary;* III: *The Roman Epistle-Lectionary.* ACC 28,
30, 32 (London 1930, 1934, 1935).
H.11.3
Capelle, B. 'L'Oeuvre liturgique de S. Gélase,' *JTS* n.s. 2 (1951) 129-44.

H.11.4

Huglo, M. 'Le Chant "vieux-romain," liste des MSS et témoins indirects,' *SE* 6 (1954) 96-124.

H.11.5

Chavasse, A. 'Liturgie papale et liturgies presbytérales: Leurs zones d'exercice' in *Mélanges Andrieu* (see **A.4.9**) 103-12.

H.11.6

Dekkers, E. 'Autour l'oeuvre liturgique de Saint Léon le Grand,' *SE* 10 (1958) 363-98.

H.11.7

Van Dijk, S.J.P. 'The Urban and Papal Rites in Seventh and Eighth-Century Rome,' *SE* 12 (1961) 411-87.

H.11.8

Van Dijk, S.J.P. 'The Old Roman Rite' in *Studia patristica,* V. Texte und Untersuchungen 80 (Berlin 1962) 185-205; and 'Recent Developments in the Study of the Old Roman Rite' in *Studia patristica,* VIII. Texte und Untersuchungen 93 (Berlin 1966) 299-319.

H.11.9

Willis, Geoffrey G. *Essays in Early Roman Liturgy.* ACC 46 (1964); and *Further Essays in Early Roman Liturgy.* ACC 50 (London 1968).

H.11.10

Van Dijk, S.J.P. 'The Medieval Easter Vespers of the Roman Clergy,' *SE* 19 (1969-70) 261-363.

H.11.11

Shepherd, M.H., Jr. 'The Liturgical Reform of Damasus I' in *Kyriakon* (see **C.5.7**) II, 847-63.

H.11.12

Cabié, Robert, ed. *La Lettre du pape Innocent Ier à Décentius de Gubbio (19 Mars 416).* Bibliothèque de la RHE 58 (Louvain 1973) R: *Bulletin de littérature ecclésiastique* 80 (1979) 49-50: A.-G. Martimort.

Roman Stational Liturgy

Cf. Morin **H.9.4.**

H.12.1
Grisar, Hartmann. *Das Missale im Lichte römischer Stadtgeschichte: Stationen, Perikopen, Gebräuche* (Freiburg 1925).

H.12.2
Kirsch, Johann P. *Die Stationskirchen des* Missale Romanum. Ecclesia orans 19 (Freiburg 1926).

H.12.3
Hierzegger, R. '*Collecta* und *Statio:* Die römischen Stationsprozessionen im frühen Mittelalter,' *ZKT* 60 (1936) 511-54.

H.12.4
Salmon, P. 'La Répartition de l'office entre les diverses églises urbaines du ve au viiie siècle,' *La Maison-Dieu* no. 27 (1951) 114-36.

H.12.5
Mohrmann, C. 'Statio,' *Vigiliae Christianae* 7 (1953) 221-45.

H.12.6
Willis, Geoffrey G. 'Roman Stational Liturgy' in *Further Essays* (see **H.11.9**) 1-88.

Anglo-Saxon

Cf. Gneuss **D.7.14.**

H.13.1
Bannister, H.M., ed. 'Liturgical Fragments. A) Anglo-Saxon Sacramentaries,' *JTS* 9 (1907-8) 398-411; and 'Fragments of an Anglo-Saxon Sacramentary,' *JTS* 12 (1910-11) 451-4.

H.13.2
Greenwell, William, ed. *The Pontifical of Egbert, Archbishop of York A.D. 732-766.* Surtees Society 27 (London 1853)
The attribution to Egbert is highly dubious.

H.13.3
Wilson, Henry A., ed. *The Calendar of St. Willibrord.* HBS 55 (London 1918)

Cf. W. Levison, 'A propos du calendrier de S. Willibrord,' *RB* 50 (1938) 37-41.
H.13.4
Stevenson, Joseph, ed. *The Latin Hymns of the Anglo-Saxon Church.* Surtees Society 23 (London 1851).
H.13.5
Warren, Frederick E., ed. *The Leofric Missal* (Oxford 1883; repr. Farnborough 1968)
Despite its name, a book of Lotharingian origin adapted for use at the cathedral church of Exeter.
H.13.6
Birch, Walter de Gray, ed. *Liber vitae: Register and Martyrology of New Minster and Hyde Abbey, Winchester.* Hampshire Record Society 5 (London 1892).
H.13.7
Frere, Walter H., ed. *The Winchester Troper.* HBS 8 (London 1894).
H.13.8
Wilson, Henry A., ed. *The Missal of Robert of Jumièges.* HBS 11 (London 1896).
H.13.9
Rule, Martin, ed. *The Missal of St. Augustine's Abbey, Canterbury* (Cambridge 1896)
The extensive introduction is a masterpiece of misplaced ingenuity.
H.13.10
Wilson, Henry A., ed. *The Benedictional of Archbishop Robert.* HBS 24 (London 1903)
This would be more correctly characterized as a pontifical.
H.13.11
Gasquet, Francis A. and Edmund Bishop. *The Bosworth Psalter* (London 1908)
A series of studies on this Anglo-Saxon psalter (London, B.L. Add. 37517) rather than an edition.
H.13.12
Warner, George F. and H.A. Wilson, eds. *The Benedictional of St. Aethelwold.* Facsimile ed. for the Roxburghe Club (Oxford 1910).
H.13.13
Dewick, E.S., ed., with W.H. Frere. *The Leofric Collectar.* 2 vols. HBS 45, 56 (London 1914, 1921).

H.13.14
Woolley, Reginald M., ed. *The Canterbury Benedictional.* HBS 51 (London 1917).
H.13.15
Lindelöf, U., ed. *Rituale ecclesiae Dunelmensis: The Durham Collectar.* Surtees Society 140 (London 1927)
Replaces the edition by J. Stevenson, Surtees Society 10 (1841).
H.13.16
Wormald, Francis, ed. *English Kalendars before A.D. 1100.* HBS 72 (London 1934).
H.13.17
Doble, George H., ed. *Pontificale Lanaletense.* HBS 74 (London 1937)
Originally used in the sub-diocese of St. Germans in Cornwall.
H.13.18
Symons, Thomas, ed. and tr., *Regularis concordia.* Nelson's Medieval Texts (London 1953).
H.13.19
Hughes, Anselm, ed. *The Portiforium of Saint Wulstan.* 2 vols. HBS 89-90 (London 1958-60).
H.13.20
Turner, Derek H., ed. *The Missal of the New Minster, Winchester.* HBS 93 (London 1962)
R: *RB* 73 (1963) 159: P. Verbraken.
H.13.21
Turner, Derek H., ed. *The Claudius Pontificals.* HBS 97 (London 1971)
R: *ALW* 16 (1974) 401-2: A. Kurzeja.
H.13.22
Wilson, H.A. 'Notes on Some Liturgical Questions Relating to the Mission of St. Augustine' in *The Mission of St. Augustine,* ed. Arthur J. Mason (Cambridge 1897) 235-52.
H.13.23
Willis, Geoffrey G. 'Early English Liturgy from Augustine to Alcuin' in *Further Essays* (see **H.11.9**) 189-243.
H.13.24
Korhammer, P.M. 'The Origin of the Bosworth Psalter,' *Anglo-Saxon England* 2 (1973) 173-87.
H.13.25
Hohler, C. 'Some Service Books of the Later Saxon Church' in *Tenth-*

Century Studies, ed. David Parsons (London 1975) 60-83 and 217-27
Highly provocative.
H.13.26
Korhammer, Michael. *Die monastischen Cantica im Mittelalter und ihre altenglischen interlinear Versionen.* Münchener Universitäts-Schriften 6 (Munich 1976)
R: *Speculum* 54 (1979) 162-4: C. Waddell.
H.13.27
Enrique Planchart, Alejandro. *The Repertory of Tropes at Winchester.* 2 vols. (Princeton 1977)
R: *Etudes grégoriennes* 17 (1978) 231-2: J. Hourlier.

Carolingian

Cf. Angenendt **E.10.5**, Amalarius **F.19.2**, and articles by Amiet, Barré, and Deshusses: **H.5.4, 12, 13, 14, 15, 16, 21.**

H.14.1
Metzger, Max J., ed. *Zwei karolingische Pontifikalien vom Oberrhein* (Freiburg 1914)
H.14.2
Unterkircher, Franz, ed. *Das Kollektar-Pontificale des Bischofs Baturich von Regensburg (817-48).* SF 8 (Fribourg 1962)
R: *EL* 77 (1963) 62-4: V. Raffa.
H.14.3
Barré, Henri. *Les Homéliaires carolingiens de l'école d'Auxerre: Authenticité, inventaire, tables comparatifs, initia.* ST 225 (Rome 1962)
R: *EL* 78 (1964) 70-74: F. Dell' Oro.
H.14.4
Netzer, H. *L'Introduction de la messe romaine en France sous les Carolingiens* (Paris 1910; repr. Farnborough 1968).
H.14.5
Wilmart, A. and E. Bishop. 'La Réforme liturgique de Charlemagne,' *EL* 45 (1931) 186-207. French translation and expansion by Wilmart of Bishop's 'The Meaning and Value of the Liturgical Reform of Charlemagne,' *Downside Review* 38 (1919-20) 1-16.

H.14.6
Andrieu, M. 'Règlement d'Angilramne de Metz (768-91) fixant les honoraires de quelques fonctions liturgiques,' *Revue des sciences religieuses* 10 (1930) 349-69.
H.14.7
Hosp, E. 'Il sermonario di Alano di Farfa,' *EL* 50 (1936) 375-83, 51 (1937) 210-41.
H.14.8
Pelt, Jean-B. *Etudes sur la cathédrale de Metz: La Liturgie,* I (Metz 1937).
H.14.9
Hucke, H. 'Die Einführung des gregorianischen Gesanges im Frankreich,' *Römische Quartalschrift* 49 (1954) 172-87.
H.14.10
Ellard, Gerald. *Master Alcuin, Liturgist: A Partner of our Piety* (Chicago 1956)
Important review by Christopher Hohler, *JEH* 8 (1957) 222-6.
H.14.11
Vogel, C. 'La Réforme liturgique sous Charlemagne' in *Karl der Grosse,* II: *Das geistige Leben,* ed. W. Braunfels (Düsseldorf 1966) 217-32.
H.14.12
Vogel, C. 'S. Chrodegang et les débuts de la romanisation du culte en pays franc' in *Saint Chrodegang* (Metz 1967) 91-109.
H.14.13
Vogel, C. 'Les Echanges liturgiques entre Rome et les pays francs jusqu'à l'époque de Charlemagne' in *Le chiese nei regni dell' Europa occidentale e i loro rapporti con Roma sino all'800.* Settimane ... Spoleto 7 (Spoleto 1960) 185-295.
H.14.14
McKitterick, Rosamund. *The Frankish Church and the Carolingian Reforms, 789-895* (London 1977), 'The Liturgy' pp. 115-54
R: *Speculum* 53 (1978) 830-31: T.F.X. Noble.

'Roman-German' Liturgy
(c 900-1200)

General

Cf. Combaluzier E.3.3, Andrieu E.4.1.

J.1.1

Vogel, Cyrille and R. Elze, eds. *Le Pontifical romano-germanique du dixième siècle.* 3 vols. ST 226-7, 269 (Rome 1963, 1972)
R: of I-II in *Römische Quartalschrift* 61 (1966) 113-15: B. Kleinheyer; of III in *HS* 25 (1972) 227-8: M.S. Gros.

J.1.2

Meersseman, Gérard G. et al., eds. *L'Orazionale dell'arcidiacono Pacifico e il Carpsum del cantore Stefano: Studi e testi sulla liturgia del duomo di Verona dal ix all'xi secolo.* SF 21 (Fribourg 1974)
R: *Studi medievali* 3rd ser. 15 (1974) 897-901: B. Baroffio
Part ii, the *Carpsum*, is an *ordo* for the daily office at Verona, transcribed about 1050 from a document written about 960.

J.1.3

Amiet, Robert, ed. *The Benedictionals of Freising.* HBS 88 (London 1974), with contributions by B.J. Wigan and C. Hohler.

J.1.4

Klauser, T. 'Die liturgischen Austauschbeziehungen zwischen der römischen und der fränkisch-deutschen Kirche vom 8. bis zum 11. Jh.,' *Historisches Jahrbuch* 53 (1933) 169-89; repr. in his *Gesammelte Arbeiten zur Liturgiegeschichte, Kirchengeschichte, und christlichen Archäologie* (Münster 1974) 139-54.

J.1.5
Turner, D.H. 'The Prayer-Book of Archbishop Arnulph II of Milan,' *RB* 70 (1960) 360-92.
J.1.6
Baroffio, B. and F. Dell' Oro. 'L' *Ordo missae* del vescovo Warmondo d'Ivrea (969-c. 1010),' *Studi medievali* 3rd ser. 16 (1975) 795-823.
J.1.7
Amiet, A. 'Die liturgische Gesetzgebung der deutschen Reichskirche in der Zeit der sächsischen Kaiser, 922-1023,' *Zeitschrift für schweizerische Kirchengeschichte* 70 (1976) 1-106, 209-307.
J.1.8
Salmon, P. 'Un *Libellus officialis* du xie siècle,' *RB* 87 (1977) 257-88.

Coronation Orders; *Laudes regiae*

Cf. Legg **L.7.1**.

J.2.1
Elze, Reinhard, ed. *Die Ordines für die Weihe und Krönung des Kaisers und der Kaiserin*. Fontes iuris Germanici antiqui in usum scholarum ex Monumentis Germaniae historicis 9 (Hannover 1960)
R: *RHE* 56 (1961) 113-16: R. Folz.
J.2.2
Legg, John Wickham, ed. *Three Coronation Orders*. HBS 19 (London 1900) Includes order for the crowning of a tenth-century Anglo-Saxon king and (in Anglo-Norman) of a fourteenth-century English king.
J.2.3
Ullmann, Walter, ed. *Liber regie capelle*. HBS 92 (London 1961)
R: *EL* 77 (1963) 62: A.P. Frutaz
On pages 74-110 is printed an 'Ordo secundum quem rex debet coronari.'
J.2.4
Dewick, E.S., ed. *The Coronation Book of Charles V of France* [1365] HBS 16 (London 1899).
J.2.5
Woolley, Reginald M. *Coronation Rites* (Cambridge 1915).
J.2.6
Bouman, Cornelius A. *Sacring and Crowning: The Development of the*

Latin Ritual for the Anointing of Kings and the Coronation of an Emperor before the Eleventh Century (Groningen 1957).
J.2.7
Schramm, Percy E. *Kaiser, Könige, und Päpste.* 4 vols. in 5 (Stuttgart 1968-71)
Volumes II and III of these collected papers make conveniently available S's monograph-length essays 'Die Krönung bei den Westfranken und Angelsachsen 878-1000' (II, 140-248) and 'Die Krönung in Deutschland bis ... 1028' (II, 287-305 and III, 59-107), first published in 1934 and 1935 respectively.
J.2.8
Schramm, Percy E. *Geschichte des englischen Königtums im Lichte der Krönung* (Weimar 1937; repr. Darmstadt 1970). ET by L.G. Wickham Legg as *A History of the English Coronation* (Oxford 1937).
J.2.9
Eichmann, Eduard. *Die Kaiserkrönung im Abendland.* 2 vols. (Würzburg 1942).
J.2.10
Mayer, Hans E. 'Das Pontifikale von Tyrus und die Krönung der lateinischen Könige von Jerusalem: Zugleich ein Beitrag zur Forschung über Herrschaftszeichen und Staatssymbolik,' *Dumbarton Oaks Papers* 21 (1967) 141-232.
J.2.11
Kantorowicz, Ernst H. *Laudes regiae: A Study in Liturgical Acclamations and Mediaeval Ruler Worship.* University of California Publications in History 33 (Berkeley 1946).
J.2.12
Knopp, G. '*Sanctorum nomina seriatim:* Die Anfänge der Allerheiligenlitanei und ihre Verbindung mit den *Laudes regiae*,' *Römische Quartalschrift* 65 (1970) 185-231.

Papal Reform

J.3.1
Cattaneo, E. 'La Liturgia nella riforma gregoriana,' *Chiesa e riforma nella spiritualità del secolo xi.* Convegni del centro di studi sulla spiritualità medievale 6 (Todi 1968) 169-90.

J.3.2
Fischer, Ludwig, ed. *Bernhardi cardinalis et Lateranensis ecclesiae prioris, ordo officiorum ecclesiae Lateranensis* (Munich 1916)
An *ordo* of the late twelfth century.
J.3.3
Peri, Vittorio. '*Nichil in ecclesia sine causa.* Note di vita liturgica romana nel xii secolo,' *Rivista di archeologia cristiana* 50 (1974) 249-73.

Cluniac

J.4.1
Bannister, H.M. 'Une tropaire-prosier de Moissac,' *Revue de l'histoire et de littérature religieuses* 8 (1903) 554-81.
J.4.2
Leroquais, Victor. *Le Bréviaire-Missel du prieuré clunisien de Lewes* (Paris 1935).
J.4.3
Hourlier, J. 'Le Bréviaire de Saint-Taurin: Un livre liturgique clunisien à l'usage de l'Echelle-Saint-Aurin,' *Etudes grégoriennes* 3 (1959) 163-73.
J.4.4
Schmitz, P. 'La Liturgie de Cluny' in *Spiritualità cluniacense.* Convegni del centro di studi sulla spiritualità medievale 2 (Todi 1960) 83-99.
J.4.5
Monterosso, R. 'Canto gregoriano e riforma tra Cluniacensi e Cistercensi' in *Chiesa e riforma nella spiritualità del secolo xi.* Convegni del centro di studi sulla spiritualità medievale 6 (Todi 1968) 191-219.
J.4.6
Etaix, R. 'Le Lectionnaire de l'office à Cluny,' *Recherches augustiniennes* 11 (1976) 91-159.

Monastic, Tenth-Twelfth Centuries

J.5.1
Hughes, Anselm, ed. *The Bec Missal.* HBS 94 (London 1963).

J.5.2

Davril, Anselm, ed. *Consuetudines Floriacenses s. xiii.* Corpus consuetudinum monasticarum 9 (Siegburg 1976)
R: *JEH* 29 (1978) 105-6: F. Hockey.

J.5.3

Pellegrin, E. 'Notes sur quelques recueils de vies de saints utilisés pour la liturgie à Fleury-sur-Loire au xie siècle,' *Bulletin d'information de l'Institut de recherches et d'histoire des textes* 12 (1963) 7-30.

Millénaire monastique du Mont Saint-Michel. 4 vols. (Paris and Nogent-sur-Marne 1966-7). See esp. in vol. I the following three articles:

J.5.4

Lemarié, J. 'La Vie liturgique au Mont Saint-Michel d'après les ordinaires et le cérémonial de l'abbaye,' I, 303-52

J.5.5

LeRoux, R. 'Guillaume de Volpiano, son cursus liturgique au Mont Saint-Michel et dans les abbayes normandes,' I, 417-72

J.5.6

Tardif, H. 'La Liturgie de la messe au Mont Saint-Michel aux xie, xiie, et xiiie siècles,' I, 353-77.

J.5.7

Lemarié, J. 'Les Formules de prières du ms. du Mont Saint-Michel, Avranches B.M. 213,' *Studi medievali* 3rd ser. 13 (1972) 1013-42.

J.5.8

Arx, Walter von, ed. *Das Klosterrituale von Biburg.* SF 14 (Fribourg 1970)
R: *JTS* n.s. 22 (1971) 631-2: R.J. Halliburton.

J.5.9

Munding, Emmanuel. *Die Kalendarien von St. Gallen ... IX-XI. Jahrhundert.* 2 vols. TA 36-7 (Beuron 1948-51).

J.5.10

Turner, D.H. 'Sacramentaries of Saint Gall in the Xth and XIth Centuries,' *RB* 81 (1971) 186-215.

J.5.11

Hänggi, Anton. *Der Rheinauer* Liber ordinarius *(Zürich Rh 80, Anfang 12. Jht.).* SF 1 (Fribourg 1957)
Prefaced by a valuable essay on *Libri ordinarii* in general.

J.5.12
Hürlimann, Gebhard. *Das Rheinauer Rituale (Zürich Rh 114, Anfang 12. Jht.).* SF 5 (Fribourg 1959).

J.5.13
Eizenhöfer, L. 'Das Lorscher Sakramentar im Cod. Vat. Pal. lat. 495' in *Die Reichsabtei Lorsch,* ed. Friedrich Knöpp, II (Darmstadt 1977) 129-69.

J.5.14
Frank, H. 'Das älteste Laacher Sakramentar' in *Enkainia ... Maria-Laach* (see **E.6.2**) 263-303.

J.5.15
Huglo, M. 'Les Livres liturgiques de la Chaise-Dieu,' *RB* 87 (1977) 62-96, 289-348.

Cistercian

Cf. *DACL* **A.2.2**, 3.ii.1779-1811; King, *Orders* **A.2.9**, 62-156; Monterosso **J.4.5.**

J.6.1
Canivez, J.M. 'Le Rite cistercien,' *EL* 63 (1949) 276-311.

J.6.2
Backaert, B. 'L'Evolution du calendrier cistercien,' *Collectanea ordinis Cisterciensium reformatorum* 12 (1950) 81-94, 302-16; 13 (1951) 108-27.

J.6.3
Marosszéki, S. 'Les Origines du chant cistercien,' *Analecta Cisterciensia* 8 (1952) 1-179.

J.6.4
Waddell, C. 'The Origin and Early Evolution of the Cistercian Antiphonary: Reflections on Two Cistercian Chant Reforms' in *The Cistercian Spirit: A Symposium,* ed. M. Basil Pennington. Cistercian Studies 3 (Spencer, Mass. 1970) 190-223.

J.6.5
Lackner, B. 'The Liturgy of Early Cîteaux' in *Studies in Medieval Cistercian History* I, ed. Joseph F. O'Callaghan. Cistercian Studies 13 (Spencer, Mass. 1971) 1-34.

J.6.6

Waddell, C. 'The Early Cistercian Experience of Liturgy' in *Rule and Life: An Interdisciplinary Symposium,* ed. M. Basil Pennington. Cistercian Studies 12 (Spencer, Mass. 1971) 77-116.

J.6.7

Huot, F. 'L'Antiphonaire cistercien au xiie siècle d'après les manuscrits de la Maigrauge,' *Zeitschrift für schweizerische Kirchengeschichte* 65 (1971) 302-414.

Carthusian

Cf. *DACL* A.2.2, 3.i.1045-71; King, *Orders* A.2.9, 1-61.

J.7.1

Hourlier, J. and B. du Moustier. 'Le Calendrier cartusien,' *Etudes grégoriennes* 2 (1957) 151-61.

J.7.2

Etaix, R. 'L'Homiliaire cartusien,' *SE* 13 (1962) 67-112.

J.7.3

Hogg, James, ed. *Mittelalterliche* Caerimonialia *der Kartäuser,* i; and *Late Fifteenth-Century Rubrics for the Deacon and the Sacristan from the MS. Valsainte 42/T.I.8.* Analecta Cartusiana 2, 4 (Salzburg 1971) R: *JEH* 23 (1972) 274-5: J.E. Sayers.

J.7.4

Becker, Hansjacob. *Die Responsorien der Kartäuserbreviers: Untersuchungen zu Urform und Herkunft des Antiphonars der Kartause.* Münchener theologische Studien, II. Systematische Abteilung 39 (Munich 1971) R: *Analecta Praemonstratensia* 51 (1975) 306-7: G. Huybens.

Premonstratensian

Cf. King, *Orders* A.2.9, 157-234.

J.8.1
Lefèvre, Placide F. *La Liturgie de Prémontré: Histoire, formulaire, chant, et cérémonial.* Bibliotheca analectorum Praemonstratensium 1 (Louvain 1957).

J.8.2
Van Waefelghem, Michel, ed. *Liturgie de Prémontré: Le* Liber ordinarius *d'après un manuscrit du xiiie-xive siècle* (Louvain 1913).

J.8.3
Lefèvre, Placide F., ed. *L'Ordinaire de Prémontré d'après des manuscrits du xiie et du xiiie siècle.* Bibliothèque de la 'Revue d'histoire ecclésiastique' 22 (Louvain 1941).

J.8.4
Lefèvre, Placide F., ed. *Coutumiers liturgiques de Prémontré du xiiie et du xive siècles.* Bibliothèque de la 'Revue d'histoire ecclésiastique' 27 (Louvain 1953; repr. 1972).

J.8.5
Weyns, N.I. 'Le Missel prémontré,' *Analecta Praemonstratensia* 43 (1967) 203-25.

J.8.6
Lefèvre, P.F. 'L'*Antiphonale psalterii* d'après le rite de Prémontré,' *Analecta Praemonstratensia* 44 (1968) 247-74.

J.8.7
Weyns, Norbert I., ed. *Sacramentarium Praemonstratense.* Bibliotheca analectorum Praemonstratensium 8 (Averbode 1968)
R: *Analecta Praemonstatensia* 47 (1971) 154: A. Verheul.

J.8.8
Weyns, Norbert I., ed. *Antiphonale missarum Praemonstratense.* Bibliotheca analectorum Praemonstratensium 11 (Averbode 1973)
R: *Analecta Praemonstratensia* 51 (1975) 183-5: A. Robeyns.

Later Medieval and Miscellaneous Monastic

J.9.1

Volk, P. 'Die erste Fassung des Bursfelder *Liber ordinarius*,' *EL* 56 (1942) 48-134.

J.9.2

Brou, Louis, ed. *The Monastic* Ordinale *of St. Vedast's Abbey, Arras.* 2 vols. HBS 86-7 (London 1957).

J.9.3

Munding, E. 'Zur Entwicklung der St. Galler Gottesdienstordnung: Die Temporalliturgie von Fridolin sicher 1520,' *Zeitschrift für schweizerische Kirchengeschichte* 55 (1961) 139-67, 309-31.

J.9.4

Becquet, J. 'La Liturgie de l'ordre de Grandmont,' *EL* 76 (1962) 146-55.

J.9.5

Saxer, V. 'Les Calendriers liturgiques de St. Victor et le sanctoral médiéval de l'abbaye,' *Provence historique* 16 (1966) 463-519.

Friars and
'Modern Roman' Liturgy

Papal Curial

K.1.1
Andrieu, M. 'Le Missel de la chapelle papale à la fin du xiiie siècle' in
Miscellanea Fr. Ehrle, II. ST 38 (Rome 1924) 348-76.
K.1.2
Van Dijk, S.J.P. 'Three Manuscripts of a Liturgical Reform by John Cajetan
Orsini (Nicholas III),' *Scriptorium* 6 (1952) 213-42.
K.1.3
Van Dijk, S.J.P. 'The Lateran Missal,' *SE* 6 (1954) 125-79.
K.1.4
Andrieu, M. 'L'Authenticité du "Missel de la chapelle papale",' *Scriptorium*
9 (1955) 17-34.
K.1.5
Van Dijk, S.J.P. 'The Legend of "the Missal of the Papal Chapel" and the
Fact of Cardinal Orsini's Reform,' *SE* 8 (1956) 76-142.
K.1.6
Van Dijk, S.J.P. 'The Authentic Missal of the Papal Chapel,' *Scriptorium*
14 (1960) 257-314.
K.1.7
Gy, P.-M. 'L'Unification liturgique de l'Occident et la liturgie de la curie
romaine,' *Revue des sciences philosophiques et théologiques* 59 (1975) 601-12.
K.1.8
Van Dijk, Stephen J.P., ed. *The Ordinal of the Papal Court from Innocent
III to Boniface VIII and Related Documents,* completed by Joan Hazelden
Walker. SF 22 (Freiburg 1975)
R: *EL* 91 (1977) 271-3: V. Raffa.

Franciscan

Cf. Van Dijk and Walker **K.5.3**, Van Dijk **K.5.4**.

For a list of Stephen J.P. van Dijk's articles, many of which pertain to the Franciscan liturgy, see the obituary by J.H. Walker, *Archivum Franciscanum historicum* 64 (1971) 591-7. Four of the most notable are given here.

K.2.1
Van Dijk, S.J.P. 'The Breviary of St. Francis,' *Franciscan Studies* n.s. 9 (1949) 13-40.
K.2.2
Van Dijk, S.J.P. 'The Liturgical Legislation of the Franciscan Rules,' *Franciscan Studies* n.s. 12 (1952) 176-95, 241-62.
K.2.3
Van Dijk, S.J.P. 'Some Manuscripts of the Earliest Franciscan Liturgy,' *Franciscan Studies* n.s. 14 (1954) 225-64, 16 (1956) 60-101.
K.2.4
Van Dijk, S.J.P. 'Ursprung und Inhalt der franziskanischen Liturgie des 13. Jahrhunderts,' *Franziskanische Studien* 51 (1969) 86-116 and 192-217.

K.2.5
Lampen, W. 'De re liturgica in opere Bartholomaei Anglici, O.F.M.,' *EL* 42 (1928) 269-84.
K.2.6
Abate, Giuseppe. 'Il primitivo breviario francescano (1224-1227),' *Miscellanea Francescana* 60 (1960) 47-240
Summarized in *EL* 76 (1962) 84-7: E. Cattaneo.
K.2.7
Desbonnets, T. 'Un Témoin de la liturgie franciscaine primitive: Meaux, Bibl. mun. 3,' *Archivum Franciscanum historicum* 63 (1970) 453-75.
K.2.8
Desbonnets, T. 'Un Rituel franciscain de 1458: Dole, Bibl. mun. 49,' *Archivum Franciscanum historicum* 65 (1972) 389-414.

Dominican

Cf. King, *Orders* A.2.9, 325-95.

K.3.1
Legg, John Wickham, ed. 'Directions for the Celebration of High Mass by the Dominican Friars from a 13th-Century MS, Brit. Mus. Add. 23935' in his *Tracts on the Mass*. HBS 27 (London 1904).

K.3.2
* Sölch, Gisbert G. *Hugo von St. Cher, O.P. und die Anfänge der Dominikaner-liturgie: Eine liturgiegeschichtliche Untersuchung zum* Speculum ecclesiae (Cologne 1938).

K.3.3
Byrnes, Aquinas, ed. *The Hymns of the Dominican Missal and Breviary* (London and St. Louis 1943).

K.3.4
Bonniwell, William R. *A History of the Dominican Liturgy* (New York 1944).

K.3.5
Bonniwell, William R., tr. *The Martyrology of the Sacred Order of Friars Preachers* (Westminster, Md. 1955).

K.3.6
Delalande, Dominique. *Vers la version authentique du graduel grégorien: Le Graduel des prêcheurs.* Bibliothèque d'histoire dominicaine 2 (Paris 1949).

K.3.7
Boyle, L.E. 'Dominican Lectionaries and Leo of Ostia's *Translatio S. Clementis,*' *Archivum fratrum praedicatorum* 28 (1958) 362-94.

K.3.8
Gleeson, P. 'Dominican Liturgical Manuscripts from before 1254,' *Archivum fratrum praedicatorum* 42 (1972) 81-135.

Carmelite

Cf. King, *Orders* A.2.9, 235-324.

K.4.1
Kallenberg, Paschalis. *Fontes liturgiae Carmelitanae.* Textus et studia historica Carmelitana 5 (Rome 1962)
R: *EL* 77 (1963) 64-7: A. Dirks.
K.4.2
Zimmerman, Benedict, ed. *Ordinaire de l'Ordre de Notre Dame du Mont-Carmel par Sibert de Beka.* Bibliothèque liturgique 13 (Paris 1910).
K.4.3
Forcadell, A. 'Ritus Carmelitarum antiquae observantiae,' *EL* 64 (1950) 5-52.
K.4.4
Rickert, Margaret. *The Reconstructed Carmelite Missal* (London 1952) Largely art-historical in approach.

'Modern Roman'

K.5.1
Lippe, Robert, ed. *Missale Romanum, Milan 1474.* HBS 17, 33 (London 1899-1907)
A useful modern edition of the *editio princeps* of a Roman missal.
K.5.2
Mohlberg, Leo Cunibert. *Radulph de Rivo, der letzte Vertreter der altrömischen Liturgie,* I: *Studien* (Louvain 1911); II: *Texte* (Münster 1911-15).
K.5.3
Van Dijk, Stephen J.P. and Joan H. Walker. *The Origins of the Modern Roman Liturgy* (London 1960)
R: *RHE* 58 (1963) 857-62: P. Lefèvre (review article).
K.5.4
Van Dijk, Stephen J.P., ed. *Sources of the Modern Roman Liturgy: The Ordinals by Haymo of Faversham and Related Documents 1243-1307.*
2 vols. Studia et documenta Franciscana 1-2 (Leiden 1963)
R: *JTS* n.s. 16 (1965) 523-6: S. Tyne.

Other Italian
(High and Late Medieval)

Cf. Grégoire A.7.1.

K.6.1
Gamber, K. 'La liturgia della diocesi dell' Italia centro-meridionale dal ix all' xi secolo' in *Vescovi e diocesi in Italia nel medioevo*. Italia sacra 5 (Padua 1964) 145-56.

K.6.2
Terrizzi, Francesco, ed. *Missale antiquum S. Panormitanae ecclesiae*. RED, series maior 13 (Rome 1970)
R: *EL* 86 (1972) 228-9: C. Braga.

K.6.3
Amiet, Robert. *Repertorium liturgicum Augustanum*. 2 vols. Monumenta liturgica ecclesiae Augustanae 1-2 (Aosta 1974)
R: *JTS* n.s. 16 (1975) 209-10: G.J. Cuming.

English Liturgy

General

Cf. King, *Past* A.2.12, 276-374; Gneuss D.7.14, Brückmann E.4.7, Dolan F.20.7, and the entire Anglo-Saxon section H.13.

L.1.1
Maskell, William. *The Ancient Liturgy of the Church of England according to the Uses of Sarum, Bangor, York, and Hereford.* 2nd ed. (London 1846; 1st ed. 1844)
The ordinary and canon of the mass according to these four 'uses' and to the modern Roman liturgy, laid out in parallel columns, with extensive, if often outdated, commentary.

L.1.2
Maskell, William. *Monumenta ritualia ecclesiae Anglicanae.* 2nd ed. in 3 vols. (Oxford 1882; repr. Farnborough 1970; 1st ed. in 2 vols. Oxford 1846)
Each volume is prefaced by a valuable 'Dissertation': on the ancient service books of the English church, I, iii-ccxxiii; on the occasional offices, I, ccxxxvi-ccclvi; on coronation rites etc., II, i-clxxx; and on the Prymer, III, i-lxvii.

L.1.3
Rock, Daniel. *The Church of our Fathers as seen in St. Osmund's Rite for the Cathedral of Salisbury.* New ed. in 4 vols. by G.W. Hart and W.H. Frere (London 1905)
The original edition, 1849-53, of this valuable but rather quirky collection of information should by no means be used.

L.1.4
Wordsworth, Christopher. *Notes on Medieval Services in England, with an Index of Lincoln Ceremonies* (London 1898).
L.1.5
Wordsworth, Christopher and H. Littlehales. *The Old Service Books of the English Church* (London 1904).
L.1.6
Dalton, John N. , with G.H. Doble, ed. *Ordinale Exon.* [Exeter Cathedral].
4 vols. HBS 37-8, 63, 79 (London 1909, 1926, 1940).
L.1.7
Woolley, Reginald M., ed. *The Benedictional of John Longlonde, Bishop of Lincoln.* HBS 64 (London 1927).
L.1.8
Pfaff, Richard W. *New Liturgical Feasts in Later Medieval England* (Oxford 1970)
R: *Medium Ævum* 40 (1971) 311-12: J.H. Crehan.

Use of Sarum

Cf. Bailey **F.18.3**, Rock **L.1.3**, Bishop **L.4.3**.

L.2.1
Legg, J [ohn] Wickham, ed. *The Sarum Missal Edited from Three Early Manuscripts* (Oxford 1916; repr. 1969).
L.2.2
Dickinson, Francis H., ed. *Missale ad usum insignis et praeclarae ecclesiae Sarum* (Burntisland 1861-83, in fascicles; repr. Farnborough 1969)
Edited from the early printed editions; difficult to use, but often more helpful than Legg's edition.
L.2.3
Warren, Frederick E., tr. *The Sarum Missal in English.* 2 vols. ACC 11 (London 1913).
L.2.4
Procter, Francis and C. Wordsworth, eds. *Breviarium ad usum insignis ecclesiae Sarum.* 3 vols. (Cambridge 1879-86; repr. Farnborough 1970)
An immensely valuable work, especially for its indices, but typographically complicated almost beyond belief.

L.2.5
Henderson, William G., ed. *Processionale ad usum insignis ac praeclarae ecclesiae Sarum*(Leeds 1882; repr. Farnborough 1969).
L.2.6
Frere, Walter H., ed. *Graduale Sarisburiense.* 2 vols. Plainsong and Medieval Music Society (London 1891-4; repr. Farnborough 1966).
L.2.7
Frere, Walter H., ed. *Antiphonale Sarisburiense.* 6 vols. Plainsong and Medieval Music Society (London 1901-15; repr. Farnborough 1966).
L.2.8
Frere, Walter H., ed. *The Use of Sarum,* I: *The Sarum Customs as set forth in the Consuetudinary and Customary;* II: *The Ordinal and Tonal* (Cambridge 1898-1901; repr. Farnborough 1969).
L.2.9
Collins, Arthur J., ed. *Manuale ad usum percelebris ecclesiae Sarisburiensis.* HBS 91 (London 1960)
R: *EL* 77 (1963) 61-2: A.P. Frutaz.
L.2.10
Procter, Francis and E.S. Dewick, eds. *The Martiloge in Englysshe after the Use of the Chirche of Salisbury and as it is Redde in Syon, with Addicyons. Printed by Wynkyn de Worde in 1526* [by Richard Whytford]. HBS 3 (London 1893).
L.2.11
Wordsworth, Christopher, ed. *The Tracts of Clement Maydeston, with the Remains of Caxton's* Ordinale [i.e. the *Ordinale Sarum*]. HBS 7 (London 1894).
L.2.12
Wordsworth, Christopher, ed. *Ordinale Sarum sive directorium sacerdotum ... auctore Clemente Maydeston.* 2 vols. HBS 20, 22 (London 1901, 1902).
L.2.13
Wordsworth, Christopher. *Ceremonies and Processions of the Cathedral Church of Salisbury.*(Cambridge 1901).
L.2.14
Legg, John Wickham, ed. *Tracts on the Mass.* HBS 27 (London 1904)
Especially for Sarum ordinaries of the 13th and 14th centuries.

Use of York

L.3.1
Henderson, William G., ed. *Missale ad usum insignis ecclesiae Eboracensis.*
2 vols. Surtees Society 59-60 (London 1874).
L.3.2
Lawley, Stephen W., ed. *Breviarium ad usum insignis ecclesiae Eboracensis.*
2 vols. Surtees Society 71, 75 (London 1880-83).
L.3.3
Henderson William G., ed. *Manuale et processionale ad usum insignis
ecclesiae Eboracensis.* Surtees Society 63 (London 1875).
L.3.4
Henderson, William G., ed. *Liber pontificalis Christopher Bainbridge archi-
episcopi Eboracensis.* Surtees Society 61 (London 1875).
L.3.5
Wordsworth, Christopher, ed. *Horae Eboracenses: The Prymer or Hours of
the Blessed Virgin Mary, according to the Use of the Illustrious Church of
York* ... Surtees Society 132 (London 1920).
L.3.6
Simmons, Thomas F., ed. *The Lay Folks Mass Book and Offices in English
according to the Use of York.* Early English Text Society o.s. 71 (London
1879)
A vernacular guide of c. 1300 to lay participation in the Mass.

Use of Hereford

L.4.1
Frere, Walter H. and L.E.G. Brown, eds. *The Hereford Breviary.* 3 vols.
HBS 26, 40, 46 (London 1904, 1911, 1915)
The introduction, in volume III, is particularly valuable for its comparisons
of Sarum, York, and Hereford breviaries.
L.4.2
Henderson, William G., ed. *Missale ad usum percelebris ecclesiae Herfordensis*
(Leeds 1874; repr. Farnborough 1969).
L.4.3
Bishop, E. 'Holy Week Rites of Sarum, Hereford, and Rouen Compared' in
Liturgica historica (see **A.4.1**) 276-300. First publ. 1894.

Scottish

L.5.1
McRoberts, David. *Catalogue of Scottish Medieval Liturgical Books and Fragments* (Glasgow 1953). Originally publ. in *Innes Review* 3 (1952) 49-63, 131-5.
L.5.2
Forbes, Alexander P. and George H. Forbes, eds. *Liber ecclesiae beati terrenani de Arbuthnott* [Arbuthnott Missal] (Burntisland 1864).
L.5.3
Blew, W.J., ed. *Breviarium Aberdonense* [Aberdeen Breviary]. 2 vols. Bannatyne Club (Edinburgh 1854).
L.5.4
Macray, W.D., ed. *Breviarium Bothanum* ['Bute' Breviary] (London 1900). Privately printed.
L.5.5
Eeles, Francis C., ed. *The Holyrood* Ordinale: *A Scottish Version of a Directory of English Augustinian Canons, with a Manual and other Liturgical Forms.* Old Edinburgh Club 7 (Edinburgh 1916).
L.5.6
Wordsworth, Christopher, ed. *Pontificale ecclesiae S. Andreae: The Pontifical Offices used by David de Bernham, Bishop of St. Andrews 1239-53* (Edinburgh 1885).

Irish (Post-1172)

L.6.1
Lawlor, Hugh J., ed. *The Rosslyn Missal, an Irish Manuscript in the Advocates' Library, Edinburgh.* HBS 15 (London 1899).
L.6.2
Warren, Frederick E., ed. *The Manuscript Irish Missal Belonging to the President and Fellows of Corpus Christi College, Oxford* (London 1879).
L.6.3
Gwynn, A. 'The Irish Missal of Corpus Christi College, Oxford' in *Studies in Church History,* ed. C.W. Dugmore and C. Duggan, I (London 1964) 47-68.

L.6.4
Forbes, George H., ed. *Missale Drummondiense: The Ancient Irish Missal in the Possession of the Baroness Willoughby de Eresby, Drummond Castle, Perthshire* (Burntisland 1882).
L.6.5
Stokes, Whitley, ed. *The Martyrology of Gorman.* HBS 9 (London 1895).

English Monastic

Cf., in the Anglo-Saxon section, Frere **H.13.7**, Rule **H.13.9**, Hughes **H.13.19**, Turner **H.13.20** and **21**.

L.7.1
Legg, John Wickham, ed. *Missale ad usum ecclesie Westmonasteriensis.* HBS 1, 5, 12 (London 1891, 1893, 1897)
This is not only the fullest and most complete edition of an English monastic missal, with valuable introduction, notes, and indices; it also contains several supplementary texts, most notably those for coronation services.
L.7.2
Jebb, Philip, ed. *Missale de Lesnes.* HBS 95 (London 1964)
For the Augustinian canons of Lesnes, Kent.
L.7.3
Tolhurst, John B.L., ed. *The Monastic Breviary of Hyde Abbey, Winchester.* 6 vols. HBS 69-71, 76, 78, 80 (London 1932-42)
Volume VI is an important 'Introduction to the English Monastic Breviaries.'
L.7.4
Wilson, Henry A., ed. *Officium ecclesiasticum abbatum secundum usum Eveshamensis monasterii.* HBS 6 (London 1893).
L.7.5
Benoît-Castelli, G. 'Un Processional anglais du xive siècle,' *EL* 75 (1961) 281-326
The 'Rollington' Processional, used by the nuns of Wilton.
L.7.6
Knowles, David, ed. and tr. *Monastic Constitutions of Lanfranc.* Nelson's Medieval Texts (London 1951).
L.7.7
Thompson, Edward Maunde, ed. *Customary of the Benedictine Monasteries*

of Saint Augustine, Canterbury and Saint Peter, Westminster. 2 vols. HBS 23, 28 (London 1902, 1904).

L.7.8

Tolhurst, John B.L., ed. *The* Ordinale *and Customary of the Benedictine Nuns of Barking Abbey*. 2 vols. HBS 65-6 (London 1927-8).

L.7.9

Gransden, Antonia, ed. *The Customary of the Benedictine Abbey of Bury St. Edmunds in Suffolk*. HBS 99 (London 1973)
R: *ALW* 17/18 (1975/76) 282: E. von Severus.

L.7.10

Fowler, J.T., ed. *Rites of Durham, Being a Description ... of all the Ancient Monuments, Rites, and Customs ... of Durham before the Suppression, Written 1593*. Surtees Society 107 (London 1903).

L.7.11

Hohler, C. 'The Durham Services in Honour of St. Cuthbert' in *The Relics of St. Cuthbert,* ed. C.F. Battiscombe (Oxford 1956) 155-91.

L.7.12

Tolhurst, John B.L., ed. *The Customary of the Cathedral Priory Church of Norwich*. HBS 82 (London 1948).

L.7.13

McLachlan, Laurentia (as the Abbess of Stanbrook) and J.B.L. Tolhurst, eds. *The Ordinal and Customary of the Abbey of St. Mary, York*. 3 vols. HBS 73, 75, 84 (London 1936, 1937, 1951).

L.7.14

Wormald, Francis. *English Benedictine Kalendars after A.D. 1100*. 2 vols. HBS 77, 81 (London 1939, 1946).

L.7.15

Wormald, Francis, 'The Liturgical Calendar of Glastonbury Abbey' in *Festschrift Bernhard Bischoff,* ed. Johannes Autenrieth and Franz Brunhölzl (Stuttgart 1971) 325-45.

L.7.16

Woolley, Reginald M., ed. *The Gilbertine Rite*. 2 vols. HBS 59-60 (London 1921-2)
Cf. King, *Orders* A.2.9, 396-409.

L.7.17

Collins, Arthur J., ed. *The Bridgettine Breviary of Syon Abbey*. HBS 96 (London 1969).

French Liturgy

General

Cf. Leroquais **C.2.3, D.1.5, D.4.1**, and **E.4.5**; Molin **E.11.2.**

M.1.1
Martène, Edmond. *De antiquis ecclesiae ritibus.* 3 vols. (Rouen 1700-02).
2nd ed. in 4 vols. (Antwerp 1736-8; repr. Hildesheim 1967); vol. IV sometimes cited as a separate work, *De antiquis monachorum ritibus*
This antique collection covers primarily French material, but it also ranges far wider.
M.1.2
Wilmart, A. 'Les Anciens Missels de la France,' *EL* 46 (1932) 235-67.
M.1.3
Oury, G. 'La Structure cérémonielle des vêpres solennelles dans quelques anciennes liturgies françaises,' *EL* 88 (1974) 336-52.

Local

Cf. many of the works listed under 'Gallican' **(G.8)** and the later Sacramentaries **(H.4-7)**.

M.2.1
Durand, Georges, ed. *Ordinaire de l'église Notre-Dame cathédrale d'Amiens par Raoul de Rouvroy (1291).* Mémoires de la Société des antiquaires de Picardie 22 (Amiens-Paris 1934).

M.2.2
Arlt, Wulf. *Ein Festoffizium des Mittelalters aus Beauvais in seiner liturgischen und musikalischen Bedeutung,* I: *Darstellungsband;* II: *Editionsband* (Cologne 1970)
R: *Speculum* 47 (1972) 742-3: H. Tischler.
M.2.3
Delaporte, Yves. *L'Ordinaire chartrain du xiiie siècle.* Société archéologique d'Eure-et Loir, Mémoires 19 (Chartres 1952-3).
M.2.4
Delaporte, Y. 'Fulbert de Chartres et l'école chartraine de chant liturgique du xie siècle,' *Etudes grégoriennes* 2 (1957) 51-81.
M.2.5
Albanès, J.H. and U. Chevalier, eds. *Institutions liturgiques de l'église de Marseille (xiiie siècle).* Bibliothèque liturgique 14 (Paris 1910).
M.2.6
Chevalier, Ulysse, ed. *Ordinaires de l'église cathédrale de Laon (xiie et xiiie siècles), suivis des deux mystères liturgiques.* Bibliothèque liturgique 6 (Paris 1897).
M.2.7
Chevalier, Ulysse, ed. *Sacramentaire et martyrologe de l'Abbaye de Saint-Rémy: Martyrologe, calendrier, ordinaires, et prosaire de la Métropole de Reims (viiie-xiiie siècles).* Bibliothèque liturgique 7 (Paris 1900)
See especially the Reims ordinal of the 12th century, edited by E. Bishop, pages 261-305.
M.2.8
Nocent, A. 'Un Fragment de sacramentaire de Sens au xe siècle: La Liturgie baptismale de la province ecclésiastique de Sens dans les manuscrits du ixe au xvie siècle' in *Miscellanea liturgica in onore di S.E. il Card. G. Lercaro,* II (Rome 1967) 649-794.
M.2.9
* Chevalier, Ulysse, ed. *Ordinaire de l'église cathédrale de Vienne (xiiie siècle).* Bibliothèque liturgique 17 (Paris 1923).

Lyons

Cf. King, *Primatial* **A.2.11**, 1-154.

M.3.1
Buenner, Denys. *L'Ancienne Liturgie romaine: Le Rite lyonnais* (Lyons 1934; repr. Farnborough 1969).
M.3.2
Combe, P.M. 'L'*Exultet* au coeur de la vigile pascale à Lyon,' *Etudes grégoriennes* 10 (1969) 125-42.

Rouen (and Normandy)

Cf. Bishop **L.4.3**, Dolan **F.20.7**.

M.4.1
Hesbert, R.-J. 'Les Manuscrits liturgiques de l'église de Rouen,' *Bulletin philologique et historique (jusqu'à 1610)* (1955-6) 441-83.
M.4.2
Collette, Amand. *Histoire du bréviaire de Rouen* (Rouen 1902).
M.4.3
Loriquet, Henri et al., eds. *Le Graduel de l'église cathédrale de Rouen au xiiie siècle.* 2 vols. (Rouen 1907).
M.4.4
Delamare, René, ed. *Le De officiis ecclesiasticis de Jean d'Avranches, archévêque de Rouen (1067-79).* Bibliothèque liturgique 22 (Paris 1923).
M.4.5
Rochais, H. 'Le Martyrologe de Saint-Ouen au xiiie siècle (Paris, BN lat. 15025),' *Recherches augustiniennes* 11 (1976) 215-84.
M.4.6
Chevalier, Ulysse, ed. *Ordinaire et coutumier de l'église cathédrale de Bayeux (xiiie siècle).* Bibliothèque liturgique 8 (Paris 1902).
M.4.7
Delamare, René, ed. *Ordo servicii de l'insigne cathédrale d'Evreux* (Paris 1924).

M.4.8

Delamare, René, ed. *Le Calendrier de l'église d'Evreux: Etude liturgique et hagiographique.* Bibliothèque liturgique 21 (Paris 1919).

Low Countries

M.5.1

Lefèvre, Placide F., ed. *Les Ordinaires des collégiales S. Pierre à Louvain et SS. Pierre-et-Paul à Anderlecht d'après des mss. du xive siècle.* Bibliothèque de la 'Revue d'histoire ecclésiastique' 36 (Louvain 1960)
R: *RHE* 56 (1961) 943-6: Y. Delaporte.

M.5.2

Lefèvre, Placide F., ed. *L'Ordinaire de la collégiale, autrefois cathédrale de Tongres, d'après un ms. du xve siècle.* 2 vols. Spicilegium sacrum Lovaniense 34-5 (Louvain 1967-8)
R: *RHE* 65 (1970) 789-97: A. Jacob, 'A propos de l'édition de l'ordinaire de Tongres.'

M.5.3

Volk, Paulus, ed. *Der Liber ordinarius des Lütticher St. Jakobs-Klosters.* Beiträge zur Geschichte des alten Mönchtums und des Benediktinerordens 10 (Münster 1923).

M.5.4

Séjourné, Paul, ed. *L'Ordinaire de S. Martin d'Utrecht.* Bibliotheca liturgica Sancti Willibrordi 1 (Utrecht 1919-21).

Other Liturgies

German

Cf. Pelt **H.14.8**, and much of section **J.1.**

N.1.1
Franz, Adolph. *Die Messe im deutschen Mittelalter: Beiträge zur Geschichte der Liturgie und des religiösen Volkslebens* (Freiburg 1902; repr. Darmstadt 1963).

N.1.2
Schönfelder, Albrecht. *Liturgische Bibliothek: Sammlung gottesdienstlicher Bücher aus dem deutschen Mittelalter,* I: *Ritualbücher* (Paderborn 1904) Includes ordinals for the dioceses of Cologne, Meissen, and Naumburg.

N.1.3
Barth, M. 'Mittelalterliche Kalendare und Litaneien des Elsass,' *Freiburger Diözesan-Archiv* 86 (1966) 352-443.

N.1.4
Farrenkopf, Edmund K. *Breviarium Eberhardi cantoris: Die mittelalterliche Gottesdienstordnung des Domes zu Bamberg.* LQF 50 (Münster 1969) R: *RHE* 65 (1970) 167-70: P. Lefèvre.

N.1.5
Lagemann, A. 'Der Festkalender des Bistums Bamberg im Mittelalter: Entwicklung und Anwendung,' *Bericht des historischen Vereins Bamberg* 103 (1967) 7-264.

N.1.6
Franz, Adolph, ed. *Das Rituale des Bischofs Heinrich I von Breslau (1302-19)* (Freiburg 1912).

N.1.7

Burr, V. 'Calendarium Elvacense,' *ALW* 6.2 (1960) 372-416.

N.1.8

Peters, Franz, J. *Beiträge zur Geschichte der Kölnischen Messliturgie: Untersuchungen über die gedruckten Missalien des Erzbistums Köln.* Colonia sacra 2 (Cologne 1951).

N.1.9

Zilliken, G. 'Die Kölner Festkalender: Seine Entwicklung und seine Verwendung zu Urkundendatierung. Ein Beitrag zur Heortologie und Chronologie des Mittelalters,' *Bonner Jahrbücher* 119 (1910) 13-157.

N.1.10

Dold, Alban, ed. *Die Konstanzer Ritualientexte in ihrer Entwicklung von 1482-1721.* LQF 5-6 (Münster 1923).

N.1.11

Reifenberg, Hermann. *Stundengebet und Breviere im Bistum Mainz seit der romanischen Epoche.* LQF 40 (Münster 1964)

R: *EL* 79 (1965) 239-40: V. Raffa

Reifenberg's complementary works, *Messe und Missalien im Bistum Mainz seit dem Zeitalter der Gotik,* LQF 37 (Münster 1960) and *Sakramente, Sakramentalien, und Ritualien im Bistum Mainz seit dem Spätmittelalter,* 2 vols., LQF 53-4 (Münster 1971-2), are mostly concerned with the postmedieval period. See *ALW* 17/18 (1975/76) 213-16: B. Mattes.

N.1.12

Stapper, R. 'Die Feier des Kirchenjahres an der Kathedrale von Münster im hohen Mittelalter,' *Zeitschrift für vaterländische Geschichte und Altertumskunde* 75 (1917) 1-181.

N.1.13

Lamott, A. 'Codex Vindobonensis 1882: Ein *Liber ordinarius* des Speyerer Domes aus dem 13. Jht.,' *Archiv für mittelrheinische Kirchengeschichte* 13 (1961) 27-48.

N.1.14

Kurzeja, Adalbert. *Der älteste* Liber ordinarius *der Trierer Domkirche.* LQF 52 (Münster 1970)

R: *EL* 86 (1972) 225-8: V. Raffa.

N.1.15

Wegner, Günter. *Kirchenjahr und Messfeier in der Würzburger Domliturgie des späten Mittelalters.* Quellen und Forschungen zur Geschichte des Bistums und Hochstifts Würzburg 22 (Würzburg 1970)

R: *Speculum* 47 (1972) 151-2: R.W. Pfaff.

Swiss

Cf. Leisibach A.7.4.

N.2.1
Huot, François, ed. *L'Ordinaire de Sion: Etude sur sa transmission manuscrite, son cadre historique, et sa liturgie.* SF 18 (Fribourg 1973)
R: *RB* 84 (1974) 420: P. Verbraken.

N.2.2
Husmann, H. 'Zur Geschichte der Messliturgie von Sitten und über ihren Zusammenhang mit den Liturgien von Einsiedeln, Lausanne, und Genf,' *Archiv für Musikwissenschaft* 22 (1965) 217-47.

N.2.3
Ladner, P. 'Ein spätmittelalterlicher *Liber ordinarius officii* aus der Diözese Lausanne,' *Zeitschrift für schweizerische Kirchengeschichte* 64 (1970) 1-103, 185-281.

N.2.4
Leisibach, J. 'Das Missale des Wilhelm Graumeister,' *Zeitschrift für schweizerische Kirchengeschichte* 71 (1977) 141-99.

Hispanic Post-1100
(i.e. Post-Mozarabic)

Cf. Szövérffy **D.7.15**, Hohler **F.13.1**, Pinell **G.6.30**.

N.3.1
Olivar, Alejandro, ed. *El sacramentario de Vich.* MHS 4 (Barcelona 1953).

N.3.2
Olivar, Alejandro, ed. *Sacramentarium Rivipullense.* MHS 7 (Madrid-Barcelona 1964)
R: *Studia monastica* 7 (1965) 231-2: J. Janini.

N.3.3
Lemarié, Joseph, ed. *Le Bréviaire de Ripoll, Paris B.N. lat. 742: Etude sur sa composition et ses textes inédits.* Scripta et documenta 14 (Montserrat 1965)
R: *Cahiers de civilisation médiévale* 10 (1967) 469-71: L. Eizenhöfer.

N.3.4

Ferreres, Juan B. *Historia del misal romano* (Barcelona 1929)
Despite its title, primarily concerned with the medieval Spanish liturgy.

N.3.5

Saxer, V. 'Manuscrits liturgiques, calendriers, et litanies des saints du xiie au xvie siècle, conservés à la Bibliothèque capitulaire de Tarazona,' *HS* 23 (1970) 335-402, 24 (1971) 367-423, 25 (1972) 131-83
Several texts are printed in the last two installments.

N.3.6

Olivar, A. 'Panorama actual de la investigació històrica de la litúrgia a Catalunya,' *Analecta sacra Tarraconensia* 41 (1968) 245-78.

N.3.7

Martimort, A.-G. 'Un Sacramentaire de la region de Carcassonne des environs de l'année 1100' in *Mélanges Andrieu* (see **A.4.9**) 305-26.

N.3.8

Janini, J. 'Los sacramentarios de Tortosa y el cambio de rito,' *Analecta sacra Tarraconensia* 35 (1962) 5-56
'Sacramentary of St. Ruf,' Tortosa, Bibl. cap. 11.

N.3.9

Olivar, A. 'El sacramentario aragonés ms. 815 de la Biblioteca de Montserrat,' *HS* 17 (1964) 61-97.

N.3.10

Mundó, A. 'El proser-troper Montserrat 73' in *Liturgica,* III. Scripta et documenta 17 (Montserrat 1966) 101-42.

N.3.11

Gros, M.S. 'El ordo romano-hispánico de Narbona para la consagración de iglesias,' *HS* 19 (1966) 321-401.

N.3.12

Gros, M.S. 'El *Missale parvum* de Vic,' *HS* 21 (1968) 313-77.

Portuguese (Braga Rite)

Cf. King, *Primatial* A.2.11, 155-285; Szövérffy D.7.15, David G.6.24.

N.4.1
Williams, H. Fulford. 'The Diocesan Rite of the Archdiocese of Braga,'
JEH 4 (1953) 123-38.
N.4.2
Bragança, J.O. 'A liturgia de Braga,' *HS* 17 (1964) 259-81
Several articles by this author have appeared in the journal *Lusitania sacra.*
N.4.3
Hughes, A. 'Medieval Liturgical Books at Arouca, Braga, Evora, Lisbon,
and Porto: Some Provisional Inventories,' *Traditio* 31 (1975) 369-84.
N.4.4
Bragança, Joaquim Oliveira, ed. *Missal de Mateus: Manuscrito 1000 da
Biblioteca pública e Arquivo distrital de Braga* (Lisbon 1975)
R: *La Maison-Dieu* no. 124 (1975) 142-4: P. Jounel.
N.4.5
Bragança, J.O., ed. 'Ritual de S. Cruz de Coimbra,' *Didaskalia* 6 (1976)
123-210; also publ. separately (Lisbon 1976).
N.4.6
Bragança, J.O. 'Pontifical de Braga do século xii: Porto, Biblioteca municipal,
ms. 1134,' *Didaskalia* 7 (1977) 309-97. French résumé, p. 342.

Scandinavian

Cf. King, *Past* A.2.12, 375-466.

N.5.1
Faehn, Helge, ed. *Fire Norske Messordninger fra Middelalderen.* Skrifter
utgitt av det Norske Videnskaps-Academi i Oslo, ii. Historisk-filosofisk
Classe 1952, no. 5 (Oslo 1953)
Includes ordinary and canon of the Roman mass from 3 manuscripts and
from the *Missale Nidrosiense* printed in 1519; English summary, pages
129-31.

N.5.2

Faehn, Helge, ed. *Manuale Norvegicum (Presta Handbók) ex tribus codicibus s. xii-xiv.* Libri liturgici provinciae Nidrosiensis medii aevi 1 (Oslo 1962)
R: *ALW* 9.2 (1966) 455: A. Kurzeja.

N.5.3

Gjerløw, Lilli, ed. *Ordo Nidrosiensis ecclesie (Ordubók).* Libri liturgici provinciae Nidrosiensis medii aevi 2 (Oslo 1968)
R: *JEH* 21 (1970) 77-9: H. Ashworth.

N.5.4

Eggen, Erik, ed. *The Sequences of the Archbishopric of Nidarós.* Bibliotheca Arnamagnaeana 21-2 (Copenhagen 1968)
R: *AB* 88 (1970) 376-9: G. Philippart.

N.5.5

Stromberg, Bengt, ed. *Missale Lundense (1514),* facsimile ed. Laurentius Petri Sällskapets Urkundsserie 4 (Malmö 1946).

N.5.6

Peters, Knut et al., eds. *Breviarium Lincopense (1493).* Laurentius Petri Sällskapets Urkundsserie 5 (Lund 1950-55, in 4 fascicles).

N.5.7

Schmid, Toni, ed. *Graduale Arosiense impressum.* Laurentius Petri Sällskapets Urkundsserie 7 (Malmö-Lund 1959-65)
R: *EL* 81 (1969) 99-100: D. Balboni.

N.5.8

Ottosen, Knud, ed. *The Manual from Notmark: Gl. kgl. Saml. 3453, 8º.* Bibliotheca liturgica Danica, series Latina 1 (Copenhagen 1970)
R: *English Historical Review* 87 (1972) 614-16: C. Hohler.

N.5.9

Ottósson, Robert A., ed. *Sancti Thorlaci episcopi officia rhythmica et proprium missae in AM 241 A Folio.* Bibliotheca Arnamagnaeana, Supplementum 3 (Copenhagen 1959).

N.5.10

Gjerløw, Lilli. *Adoratio crucis: The* Regularis concordia *and the* Decreta Lanfranci: *Manuscript Studies in the Early Medieval Church of Norway* (Oslo 1961)
R: *JTS* n.s. 14 (1963) 210: C.N.L. Brooke.

Hungarian

N.6.1
Radó, Polycarp. *Libri liturgici manuscripti bibliothecarum Hungariae et limitropharum regionum* (Budapest 1973). Replaces the 1947 work of the same title
R: *EL* 91 (1977) 235-40: A. Dirks.

N.6.2
Strittmatter, A. 'Liturgical Manuscripts Preserved in Hungarian Libraries: A Survey of Sacramentaries, Missals, Lectionaries,' *Traditio* 19 (1963) 487-507.

N.6.3
Morin, G. 'Manuscrits liturgiques hongrois des xie et xiie siècles,' *JLW* 6 (1926) 54-67.

N.6.4
Kniewald, K. 'Das Sanctorale des ältesten ungarischen Sakramentars,' *JLW* 15 ('1935,' publ. 1941) 1-22, 306.

N.6.5
Radó, P. 'De originibus liturgiae Romanae in Hungaria saeculi xi,' *EL* 73 (1959) 299-309.

Crusader (Latin East)

N.7.1
Wormald, F. 'Liturgical Note' in Hugo Buchthal, *Miniature Painting in the Latin Kingdom of Jerusalem* (Oxford 1957) 107-34.

N.7.2
Kohler, C. 'Un Rituel et un bréviaire du St.-Sépulcre de Jérusalem (xiie-xiiie siècle),' *Revue de l'Orient latin* 8 (1900-01) 383-500.

N.7.3
Braun, O. 'Der Palmsonntag in Jerusalem zur Zeit der Kreuzzüge,' *Historisch-politische Blätter für das katholische Deutschland* 171 (1923) 497-512.

Index

All references are to entry numbers. A numbers will be found on pages 3-13, B on 14-17, C on 18-25, D on 26-33, E on 34-44, F on 45-59, G on 60-71, H on 72-88, J on 89-97, K on 98-102, L on 103-7, M on 108-11, N on 112-18.

122 / Index

Berger, B.-D. F.20.8
Bernal, J. F.8.12, G.6.26
Bernard, J. G.7.5
Bernold of Constance F.19.6
Beumer, J. G.2.3
'Bibliographia liturgica' A.1.5
Birch, W. de G. H.13.6
Bishop, E. A.4.1, C.3.2, C.7.3,
   F.14.2, F.15.1, G.7.9, H.3.4,
   H.11.1, H.13.11, H.14.5, L.4.3,
   M.2.7
Bishop, W. G.6.20
Blaise, A. A.9.5
Blew, W. L.5.3
Blume, C. C.6.2-4, D.7.2, G.6.10
Bonniwell, W. K.3.4-5
Borella, P. C.8.2, G.3.12
Botte, B. B.2.3, C.3.1, C.7.1, F.4.1;
   Festschrift to A.4.10
Bouman, C. J.2.6
Bourque, E. H.1.3, H.4.9, H.5.9
Bouyer, L. A.3.4
Boyle, L. K.3.7
Bragança, J. N.4.2, N.4-6
Brandolini, L. E.7.8
Braun, O. N.7.3
Brightman, F. B.4.1
Brinkhoff, L. A.1.2
Brinktrine, J. C.3.6, H.6.3
Brou, L. C.4.6, D.4.2, G.6.9, G.6.14,
   G.6.16, H.5.11, J.9.2
Browe, P. C.7.5, C.8.1, C.10.2,
   E.13.2, E.14.4, F.9.6, F.11.1-2
Brown, L. L.4.1
Brückmann, J. E.4.7
Bruylants, P. C.4.1
Buenner, D. M.3.1
Bulst, W. D.7.10

Burr, V. N.1.7
Byrnes, A. K.3.3

Cabié, R. F.9.4, H.11.12
Cabrol, F. A.1.1, A.2.2, A.8.2,
   A.10.1, B.5.1, C.1.4, G.4.3
Cagin, P. G.3.8, H.4.3
Callewaert, C. A.4.3, C.3.4, D.2.1,
   E.14.5, F.3.2, F.5.3, H.2.4
Canal, J. F.15.5, F.16.3
Canivez, J. J.6.1
Capelle, B. A.4.6, C.3.3, C.3.7-8,
   C.4.3, E.14.2, F.8.6, F.14.4-5,
   H.2.3, H.3.7, H.11.3
Casel, O. E.8.1
Cattaneo, E. J.3.1
Chambers, E. F.20.1
Chapman, J. H.9.2
Chavasse, A. C.5.5, E.9.7, F.5.4-5,
   H.2.6, H.3.6, H.4.10, H.11.5
Chevalier, U. D.7.1, H.7.1, M.2.5-7,
   M.2.9, M.4.6
Claire, J. D.6.5
Coebergh, C. E.9.9, H.2.7, H.5.19
Colette, M.-N. F.10.4
Collette, A. M.4.2
Collins, A. L.2.9, L.7.17
Combaluzier, F. E.3.3, G.3.6
Combe, P. M.3.2
Connelly, J. D.7.11
Coppo, A. G.1.5
Corbett, J. F.19.11
Cottiaux, J. F.11.6
Couratin, A. C.7.9
Croce, W. F.4.3
Crocker, R. C.6.11
Cross, F. A.2.1
Cullmann, O. F.4.6

Toronto Medieval Bibliographies

Editor: John Leyerle
Centre for Medieval Studies, University of Toronto

1
Old Norse-Icelandic Studies
Hans Bekker-Nielsen, Editor, *Mediaeval Scandinavia,* Co-editor of
Bibliography of Old Norse-Icelandic Studies and of *Den Arnamagnæanske
Kommissions Ordbog,* Odense University

2
Old English Literature
Fred C. Robinson, Department of English, Yale University

3
Medieval Rhetoric
James J. Murphy, Chairman, Department of Rhetoric,
University of California (Davis)

4
Medieval Music: The Sixth Liberal Art
Andrew Hughes, Faculty of Music, University of Toronto

5
Medieval Celtic Literature
Rachel Bromwich, University Reader in Celtic Languages and Literature,
University of Cambridge

6
Medieval Monasticism
Giles Constable, Director, Dumbarton Oaks

7
La Littérature occitane du moyen âge
Robert A. Taylor, Department of French, Victoria College,
University of Toronto